NO-LIMIT
TEXAS
HOLD'EM

The New Player's Guide to Winning
Poker's Biggest Game

ABOUT THE AUTHORS

World Series of Poker Champions Tom McEvoy and Brad Daugherty are among the greatest tournament poker players today. They have won millions of dollars playing tournaments against the very best in the world.

McEvoy, the 1983 World Champion of Poker, has won four World Series titles. He is the author of the acclaimed *Championship Tournament Poker,* "one of the most important poker books of all time" according to Gamblers Book Club in Las Vegas, and co-author of seven other titles: *Championship No-Limit & Pot-Limit Hold'em, Championship Stud, Championship Omaha, Championship Satellite Strategy, The Championship Table, Championship Tournament Practice Hands* and *Championship Hold'em.*

Daugherty, the 1991 World Champion of Poker, was the first player in World Series of Poker history to win $1 million. Two years after winning the title, he came close again, appearing at the championship table at the 1993 World Series of Poker. He has won countless tournaments and is one of the most feared poker players today in both brick-and-mortar and online tournaments. Daugherty is the co-author of *Championship Satellite Strategy.*

NO-LIMIT TEXAS HOLD'EM

The New Player's Guide to Winning
Poker's Biggest Game

Brad Daugherty • Tom McEvoy

CARDOZA PUBLISHING

Cardoza Publishing is the foremost gaming and gambling publisher in the world with a library of more than 100 up-to-date and easy-to-read books and strategies. These authoritative works are written by the top experts in their fields and with more than 7,000,000 books in print, represent the best-selling and most popular gaming books anywhere.

FIRST CARDOZA EDITION

Copyright©2004 by Brad Daugherty, Tom McEvoy & Dana Smith
- All Rights Reserved -

Library of Congress Catalog Card No: 2004101292
ISBN:1-58042-148-2

The authors can be emailed at: brad@bradpoker.com
                                  tommcevoy@cox.net

Editorial consultant: Dana Smith   pokerbooks@cox.net

Visit us at www.cardozapub.com or write to the address below for a full list of Cardoza books, advanced, and computer strategies.

CARDOZA PUBLISHING
P.O. Box 1500 Cooper Station, New York, NY 10276
Phone (800)577-WINS
email: cardozapub@aol.com
www.cardozapub.com

The Story Behind the Photo

The money pictured on the front cover is the actual $1 million that Brad Daugherty won at the World Series of Poker in 1991 when he became the first World Champion of Poker to win a million dollars. Stacked on top of the money are the K♠ J♠ that he played in the final hand to defeat Don Holt's 7♠ 3♠ and win the tournament. For complete details on how Daugherty won the title, read Tom McEvoy's play-by-play account in *The Championship Table*.

The 1984 World Series of Poker brochure featured Tom McEvoy as the reigning World Champion of Poker. The four photos in the insert were taken of past champions when they received the cash for their victory. Doyle Brunson (top left), won back-to-back championships in 1976-77. Stu Ungar (top right with Jack Binion) won back-to-back championships in 1980-81 and won a third championship in 1997. Hal Fowler (bottom left) won the championship in 1979. Jack Straus (bottom right) won the championship in 1982.

TABLE OF CONTENTS

PART FIVE
Determining How Much to Bet:
The Second Winning Skill of No-Limit Hold'em . 49

PART SIX
Understanding Your Opponents:
The Third Winning Skill of No-Limit Hold'em... 65

PART SEVEN
Knowing When and How to Bluff:
The Fourth Winning Skill of No-Limit Hold'em . 71

Foreword

by Barry Shulman

You might have thought it would've happened before now. I mean, it was bound to have been done sooner or later. But who could have predicted that it would take so many years for someone—let alone *these* someones—to write the definitive how-to guide to no-limit hold-em?

Since it's always been associated with the most famous gamblers playing for the highest stakes in poker's biggest games, no-limit hold'em has traditionally been known as the Rolls Royce of poker games. Until recently, however, virtually all poker games played in the United States have been limit poker, where the size of one's bet is pre-established. No-limit is more complicated because, in addition to deciding whether to bet or raise, there's the added consideration of exactly how much money to push into the pot.

Today, thanks to technology and the media, poker is booming! More than a million people watch poker on television each week, while the same number of folks are playing daily on the Internet, in poker rooms and in home games. Now no-limit hold'em is being spread (that's poker-speak for "games are being dealt") at all levels, even the smallest ones. It simply stands to reason that this rising interest is coming from new, inexperienced players who are spearheading a resurgence in a fun and exciting pastime that, in the words of my son, is "as old-school as they come."

Warning: Watching televised tournaments is *not* how you learn to win! Those tournaments you see with their huge stakes and high antes are short-handed bluffing games. They definitely are not the norm. There should be a warning that flashes across the screen during televised events: "Beginners beware—do not try this at home!" That alone is a good enough reason to invest in this book.

Where *No-Limit Texas Hold'em* differs from many other poker books is the clear and easy-to-comprehend manner in which it is written, a style that makes it the ideal primer for the novice poker player. World champions both, Brad Daugherty and Tom McEvoy are two of the only guys I know of who really are able to put their money where their mouths are. And they do it here like the pros they are.

Read the book. You'll be glad you did. I was.

Barry Shulman, the publisher of Card Player Magazine, won a gold bracelet at the 2001 World Series of Poker for his first-place finish in the $1,500 buy-in seven-card stud split tournament. That same year, he won the $5,000 buy-in no-limit hold'em championship at the Four Queens Classic. Shulman also won the $540 buy-in no-limit hold'em tournament at Jack Binion's World Poker Open in 2000. In 2003 he won the $1,500 buy-in no-limit hold'em tournament at Bellagio's Five Diamond World Poker Classic. Shulman also has appeared on television at the final table of the World Poker Tour.

Introduction

by Dana Smith

Whether you are an experienced limit poker player who wants to learn to play no-limit hold'em—or you're a rookie who has never played a single hand of hold'em—*No Limit Texas Hold'em* will guide you to the winners' circle far faster than you ever imagined.

Brad Daugherty, the 1991 World Champion of Poker, has teamed with Tom McEvoy, the 1983 World Champion of Poker, to teach you how to play poker's hottest game. Remembering the days when he first began playing poker in his Idaho hometown, Daugherty decided that, because of the exposure that has come from televised tournaments, a lot of people who have never played a hand of poker in their lives would probably like to try playing no-limit hold'em.

And so, he wrote a special section, "Brad's Crash Course in No-Limit Hold'em for Total Beginners." If you have never played poker before, read and study Part One first.

If you're an experienced hold'em player who is making a transition to no-limit play, start by reading Part Two, in which the authors advise you on how to adjust to no-limit hold'em. The champs follow up by outlining the winning principles of no-limit Texas hold'em in Part Three, and then fill in the blanks in Part Four by teaching you the four major skills you must master to win at no-limit hold'em.

If you have been reluctant to try playing no-limit hold'em because it seems such a challenge to figure out how much you should bet, you will especially benefit from Part Five, "Determining How Much to Bet," and the Betting Charts on pages 60-61. These betting charts are the first ever to be published. We think that the charts alone may be enough to give many of you the confidence you need to venture into the exciting world of no-limit hold'em tournaments.

To illustrate the general principles of no-limit play, Daugherty and McEvoy give you specific how-to advice by picturing tournament practice hands and suggesting the best way to play them before and after the flop. As an added bonus, they have set up special bluffing scenarios with practice hands designed to help you understand the art and science of bluffing.

They also provide you with their proven strategies and experience-based expertise on how to play online and on-land no-limit hold'em cash games. In Part Eleven you will find practice hands for the low-limit cash games that are offered daily at online cardrooms and now are being spread in some brick and mortar casinos.

Tournament no-limit hold'em is the playground of the world's most famous poker players. Daugherty and McEvoy have been playing in that world for many years. One of their goals in writing this book is to teach you the skills you need to join the elite ranks of million-dollar, no-limit hold'em tournament winners—the players that you've seen in televised tournaments pushing mountains of chips into the middle of the table as though they were playing with Monopoly money.

The authors sincerely believe that by using the advice in this book, you can join the game with confidence—knowing that with knowledge, skill, practice and a little bit of luck, you can conquer it. Brad and Tom are looking forward to shaking your hand at the championship table one day very soon.

PART ONE

Brad's Crash Course in No-Limit Hold'em for Total Beginners

If you are an experienced hold'em player, you do not need to read this part. We have designed it specifically for people who have never played hold'em poker. If that's you, study this chapter in detail. We also suggest that you study the Glossary of Poker Terms and refer to it while you are reading this chapter.

How No-Limit Hold'em Is Played

Each player is dealt two cards face down, beginning with the player sitting to the left of the *button*. The button is a small disc that indicates who the "dealer" is. It is used by the casino dealer so that he can keep track of who the dealer would be if players dealt the cards themselves like they used to do in the old days of casino poker and the way people still do in home games.

At the start of every new deal, the casino dealer moves the button one seat to the left.

Posting the Blinds

The first person to the left of the button is called the *Small Blind* and must post a predetermined bet in front of him before the deal. The second person to the left of the button is called the *Big Blind.* The Big Blind must post a prescribed bet before the deal that is double the amount of the Small Blind. The purpose of posting blind bets is to stimulate action. That is, the blinds get the pot started so that there will be some money to fight over. The blinds force people to play a variety of hands that they might not have otherwise entered the pot with.

In cash games the amount of money that you must post when it's your turn to be the Big Blind or the Small Blind remains the same throughout the game. In tournaments, the amount of money that you must post when it's your turn to be the Big Blind or the Small Blind increases at the beginning of each new *round.* A tournament round is a predetermined length of time during which the blinds remain the same.

In some tournaments, a round remains at the same level of blinds for only twenty minutes. In others, the rounds may stay the same for one hour or more. If you

The Set-Up of a No-Limit Hold'em Game

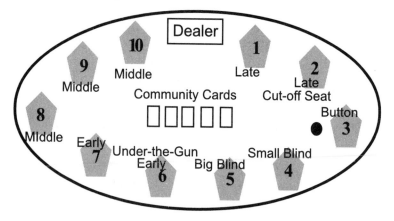

never play a hand, you will eventually go broke just from putting in the two blind bets that you are forced to post.

Posting an Ante

In some tournaments each player also must post an ante on every hand in the betting round. The ante is much smaller than either of the two blind bets. The purpose of the ante is to involve every player in the hand and to make the pot bigger. (Antes usually are not used in cash games.)

When it gets to the final six players in the World Poker Tour or the final nine players at the World Series of Poker, the forced blind bets and the antes are so high that players cannot just sit there waiting for the best hands. If they are short on chips, they absolutely have to play a hand, even if it isn't as good a hand as they want.

The Goal of Each Hand

The goal of each hand is to win the pot. You do this by having the best hand at the showdown, or by bluffing your opponents. You choose the best five-card poker hand by using any combination of your hole cards and the community cards. Your best hand can be any combination of none, one, or both of your cards with the cards in the middle.

Look at it as having a seven-card hand, from which you choose the best five-card combination. If a royal flush comes out in the middle (the community cards), everybody remaining in the hand has a royal flush because that is the best hand possible. Or if the board cards come with K♠ Q♠ J♠ 10♠ and you have the A♠ in your hand, you have a royal flush and nobody else has one.

You might also win by bluffing—representing to your

opponents that you have the A♠ in your hand—if you bet an amount of chips that no one dares call for fear that you have them beaten. You often see players make bluff bets on televised events.

The Four Betting Rounds

The first round of betting begins after you have been dealt two *hole* cards (your *hand*). The first player to act is the person immediately to the left of the Big Blind. The action continues clockwise with everyone acting in turn and the Big Blind being the last player to act.

Then the dealer puts three community cards (the *flop*) face up in the center of the table and the second round of betting begins. Starting with the first player to the left of the button who is still in the hand, each player who did not fold before the flop can check, bet, call a bet, raise, reraise or fold to a bet when it is his turn to act.

The dealer then places a fourth community card (called *fourth street* or the *turn*) face up in the center of the table, followed by another round of betting. Then he deals the final community card (called *fifth street* or the *river*) face up in the center and there is a final round of betting.

Any player can bet his entire stack of chips on any of these betting rounds. In no-limit hold'em, when a player wants to bet all his chips at once, he announces "I'm going all in!" and pushes all of his chips into the center of the table. If an opponent calls the all-in bet, the size of the bet can be no bigger than the smallest stack of the two players.

If the player with the biggest stack loses the hand, he keeps the remaining chips in his stack. For example, suppose player A has $6,000 in chips and goes all in against player B, who has $4,000 in chips. Player B goes on to win the pot. Player A would still have $2,000 in chips remaining.

How the Betting Goes

Suppose the amount of the Small Blind is $2,000 and the Big Blind is $4,000. The dealer has just dealt two cards to each player. He has not dealt any community cards yet. The player sitting to the immediate left of the Big Blind is the first person to act. He has to match the size of the Big Blind (*call*) if he wants to play his cards. In this example, $4,000 is the least that he can bet in order to play the hand.

If he wants to raise, he must bet at least $8,000 (double the amount of the Big Blind). He also can raise any amount up to the number of chips he has in his possession. For example, if he has $80,000 in front of him, he can raise to $30,000 by announcing "Raise to $30,000." Or he can bet his entire $80,000 by announcing "All in."

A player who does not have enough chips to call the minimum bet can still play the hand by putting in all the chips he has left. For instance, if he only has $3,000 in chips, he can call with everything he has by announcing "All in."

At the end of the fourth betting round, the player with the best hand wins all the chips in the middle of the table (the *pot*). If a player loses all of his chips in a cash game, he can reach into his pocket and put more money on the table. But if he loses all his chips in a tournament game, he is eliminated from action and must vacate his seat unless he goes broke during the rebuy period of a rebuy tournament.

Deciding How Much to Bet

It is often hard to understand why players bet a certain amount of chips. Are there some guidelines to help new players decide how much to bet? As a general rule, when you are the first person to enter the pot, we suggest that when you raise, you bet three to four times the size of the big blind. Sometimes you bet more than this, and other times you should bet all of your chips (move-in). We have included a betting chart on pages 60-61 to help you decide the correct amount to bet.

The Types of Hands to Play

In no-limit hold'em, big pairs and high cards rule. Two aces, two kings, two queens, two jacks, and A-K are premium hands. You would like to have a pair in your hand and then see one of your rank come on the flop. If you have two queens in your hand and a queen comes on the flop, you have made three queens to start with (a *set*). Or, if you have the A♣ K♣ and three clubs come on the flop, you have flopped a flush, which is the best possible hand (the *nuts*).

If you have the A♣ K♣ and the J♣ 4♣ 8♥ come on the flop, you have the *nut* flush draw. Then if another club comes on the turn or river, you will make the nut flush. You might also flop a pair. Suppose the flop comes K♥ 6♣ 4♣ and you are holding the A♣ K♣. You would have top pair—two kings with an ace kicker—and the nut flush draw, which is a very powerful hand.

Other hands are also playable under the right circumstances, but the above mentioned premium hands are the ones that you would prefer playing.

Reading the Board Cards

When you're playing hold'em, it is very important for you to be able to read the board in order to determine what the best possible hand is with every community card that is dealt. It is impossible, for example, for anyone to have a full house or four of a kind unless the board is paired. If you have made a straight or a flush, you can easily decide whether it is the best possible straight or flush.

You should always ask yourself, "What, at this moment, is the best possible hand?" The answer can change with every card that comes out in the middle. For example, if you start with two aces in your hand, you have the nuts before the flop. Then, depending on the cards that are dealt on the flop, the value of your hand may change.

If you have two cards of the same suit in your hand and three cards in your suit come on the flop, you have made a flush, which probably is the best possible hand at the moment unless someone else has two higher cards in your suit. Then if the board pairs on the turn, your flush may no longer be the best hand because it is possible that someone else has made a full house. (However, just because the board pairs doesn't mean that your flush is beaten.)

Here's another example. If the flop comes K♣ Q♦ 2♣ and you have K♠K♥, you have the nuts on the flop. But the turn card could change the whole scenario. Another club could come on the turn, giving somebody else a flush. Or another card (such as a ten) could be dealt that makes a straight for an opponent who has the A♦ J♥ in his hand, which would also beat your three kings.

The Bottom Line

Reading the board correctly plays an important role in determining the value of your hand. Understanding the value of your hand is important in deciding whether to bet, fold, call or raise. Betting the correct amount of chips when you are the first player to act, folding when you know you should, just calling the opening bet, and raising the appropriate amount when the time is right are skills that are unique to no-limit poker. When you have mastered selecting the best hands to play, reading the board correctly, understanding the value of your hand, knowing when to bluff, and determining the correct amount to bet, you are on your way to becoming a winning no-limit hold'em player.

PART TWO

Shifting Your Thinking from Limit to No-Limit

Players who decide to expand their repertoire of poker games often make mistakes when they first start playing a new game at which they have no experience. In this chapter, our goal is to help you adjust your thinking and your strategy when you first start playing no-limit hold'em so that you will make the fewest mistakes possible in the first no-limit tournaments or cash games you play.

We realize that many limit hold'em players who decide to venture into no-limit hold'em are fearful at first. We feel safe when we know the boundaries within which we can operate—and that is why many players feel more secure in limit games. Without the structure of limits, you may feel lost, as though you are driving in a strange city without a road map. Limit hold'em prescribes exactly how much you can bet and how much other people can bet against you, so you know in advance how much you might risk on a hand. In no-limit hold'em, there are no such restrictions.

Whereas in limit hold'em, the amount of the bet is dictated by a predetermined limit, the only limit on how much you can bet in no-limit hold'em is the amount of chips you have in front of you. You can bet all of your chips or just a few of them—and so can all the other play-

ers at your table. This freedom of choice makes many players who are accustomed to having limited choices feel uncomfortable. They sweat every betting decision. In a nutshell, limit hold'em has fixed betting limits with both a minimum and a maximum bet. In no-limit hold'em, there is a minimum bet but no maximum bet. You can bet all your chips in no-limit poker at any time.

The key to feeling comfortable in no-limit poker is getting a feel for how much you *should* bet rather than how much you *can* bet. In this book, we will give you specific instruction on how much to bet so that you can overcome your fears and feel comfortable and competent playing no-limit hold'em. Our betting chart gives you very clear guidelines on how much to bet at every stage in a tournament.

Now let us move on to some of the basic changes in thinking and strategy that you need to make in order to transition from limit hold'em to no-limit hold'em. First, you must learn to think outside the box. In a $1-$2 limit hold'em game, for example, you think inside the $1-$2 box: "I can bet $1 on the flop and $2 on the turn." In a no-limit hold'em game with $1-$2 blinds, you think outside the $1-$2 box: "I can bet a few chips, a lot of chips, or all my chips."

In limit hold'em, the size of the game is determined by the limit on how much you can bet. In no-limit hold'em, the size of the game is determined by the size of the blinds. A no-limit hold'em game with $1-$2 blinds can be a much bigger game than a limit hold'em game with $1-$2 blinds because you can bet all your chips any time you wish.

Any time you play a hand in no-limit hold'em, you could be putting all your chips at risk. You have to learn

how to manage the amount of chips you put at risk. There is no disgrace in going broke on a hand. It is far more common in no-limit poker than it is in limit poker.

Some hands that you can play in limit hold'em should be avoided almost entirely while you are making your transition to no-limit hold'em. Hands such as 6-5, 8-7, and 10-9 suited—drawing hands where you have to call with a large percentage of your chips to try to make the draw—are examples of hands you should avoid playing, especially in raised pots.

Pairs from jacks down to deuces need to be played for as few chips as possible before the flop. With less than premium pairs, you're just hoping to make a set on the flop. If you make the set, you will then have a hand that warrants playing strongly, all the while taking into account the other hands that could be out against you.

There usually are fewer people in each pot in no-limit hold'em than there are in limit hold'em. You will not be playing nearly as many multiway pots in no-limit hold'em as you do in limit hold'em, especially as the blinds get higher.

You can win the pot before the flop more often in no-limit hold'em than you can in limit hold'em. Furthermore, fewer hands are played to the river in no-limit hold'em than they are in limit hold'em.

You can protect your hand by raising a large amount in no-limit hold'em, whereas you can only raise the standard amount in limit hold'em. For example, say that you are on the button with two aces. The blinds are $25-$50. The first player in the pot makes it $100 and three players call before it gets to you. In limit hold'em, all you can raise the pot to is $150. Then everyone will usually call

the extra $50, making a big pot. On the flop there is usually a flurry of action because the size of the pot is giving players who have picked up draws the proper odds to call bets and raises.

In no-limit hold'em, you can protect your hand by raising enough chips before the flop to eliminate some players who otherwise might have called a smaller bet. In this way, you limit the field and give your aces a better chance of holding up. In the limit hold'em example where four players had put in $100 each, you could raise only $50 more.

But in no-limit hold'em, you could raise to $400 or more. Now your opponents are put to the test as to whether they want to play with you with a somewhat mediocre hand. Whereas the pot was giving our limit hold'em players good enough odds to call before the flop to try to make their drawing hands, you can put much more pressure on your opponent(s) after the flop by betting enough to make it unprofitable for them to go for their draws.

The bluff is far more important in no-limit hold'em than it is in limit hold'em. The ability to make a large enough bet to make your opponents fold all but their strongest hands is, in fact, a key factor in your no-limit hold'em success. In limit poker, since the most you can bet at one time is limited, your opponents will call your bluff bets more often. Learning when to bluff—timing your bluffs correctly—can mean the difference in winning or losing.

Understanding your opponents is critical to your success at no-limit hold'em. In fact it is even more important than it is in limit hold'em. If you make a mistake in a limit hold'em tournament, you may lose a few extra bets. In no-limit hold'em, you can lose your entire stack by

making one wrong move. If you can read your opponents correctly, you can make very good calls when you know that someone is out of line, or fold a hand when you are sure that you are beaten. Understanding your opponents also helps you decide when the time is right to attempt a bluff, and detect bluffs that you suspect your opponents are making.

The Story Behind the Photo

Brad Daugherty has a straight face here, but trust us, he's feeling pretty good. That's the champ's money.

PART THREE

The 8 Winning Principles
of No-Limit Hold'em

Certain basic principles of no-limit hold'em form the cornerstone of successful strategy. If you understand these concepts before you begin playing no-limit hold'em, many of your strategy decisions will fall into place automatically. Always keep the following principles in mind while you are playing the game and you will progress from beginner to winner far more rapidly than you ever imagined.

1. You Need a Stronger Hand to Call With than You Need to Bet With

When you are the first player in the pot and come in for a raise, you put your opponents to the test. If they are smart, they realize that they need a stronger hand to call with than you need to bet with. Conversely, if an opponent moves in on you, you must have a hand in order to justify calling. Although he doesn't need to have a hand to raise, you need to have a hand to call his raise.

When somebody moves in, decide how strong you think his hand might be. If you think that your opponent is out of line, you sometimes might call with a somewhat weaker hand. Suppose you have an A-Q, for example.

You might consider calling if you think the raiser is just trying to put a move on you. He may be going all in, for instance, because he is shortstacked and wants to try to improve his chip position by blowing you out of the pot.

When you are so short on chips that you have plummeted into the "all-in stack" range on our betting chart (pages 60-61), you are more likely to take a risk by raising with a hand such as middle suited connectors—but only when you are the first one in the pot and can make a big enough raise to get your opponents to lay down their hands. This is why we say that when you are first to act, you can raise with a weaker hand than you can call with. As the first bettor in the pot, you put your opponent(s) to the test—but when an opponent is the first one in the pot, he puts you to the test.

2. You Don't Need to Win a Lot of Pots

In limit hold'em you have to win a series of hands to be successful, but in no-limit you only have to win certain key hands. This is true because the pots that you win in no-limit play are often much bigger than they are in limit games. Either your whole stack or your opponent's whole stack can go into the pot during a hand. And when the money goes in, you want to have the best hand.

3. You Do Not Play as Many Drawing Hands

In no-limit it is usually too expensive to put in all your chips with only a drawing hand, whereas in limit hold'em you usually can draw far more cheaply. You will win far more no-limit hold'em pots before the flop and on the flop than you do in limit hold'em. This happens because drawing to a hand in limit hold'em will cost you only a prescribed number of bets, whereas taking a draw in no-limit hold'em can cost you your entire stack. Also, with fewer players in most no-limit hold'em pots, the odds are usually not favorable enough to warrant taking the draw.

4. Your Style of Play Affects Your Chances of Winning

In no-limit poker, excessively tight play doesn't cut it. It will, however, allow you to survive longer. Suppose you get to the final three or four tables and they all have you outchipped three or four to one so that you're forced to play a marginal hand. What have you accomplished? In other words, very tight play usually doesn't allow you to win tournaments because you just don't get enough premium hands, or you don't get enough action on your good hands, to accumulate enough chips to be competitive late in the tournament. You have to use a different style of play to be most effective in tournaments.

Solid-aggressive is the style that we recommend. You don't want to play a whole lot of hands, but when you do play a hand you want to be aggressive, unless you're trying to trap an opponent by just calling during the early betting rounds.

5. Getting to Know Your Opponents is Very Important

You need to stay tuned into the game every minute, watching the other players, looking for their unique mannerisms, and noting the hands they turn up at the showdown. Your mission is to get free information from them. Later in this book we discuss some ways that you can identify your opponents' betting patterns and special behaviors so that you can play correctly against them.

6. The Button Is the Position of Power

The **button**, the player tha holds the dealer's seat and is the last to act, is the position of power in no-limit hold'em. As you put more mileage under your belt, you will learn how to wield that power to bully your opponents and win some pots "without a hand" (with inferior cards), especially after the blinds have increased.

When you are the last player to bet, you are able to observe your opponents and therefore, make a more informed decision. For example, suppose you flop the nut hand. On every betting round, the other players must act before you do. Based on their actions, you can choose the best way to get the most money out of your hand.

Some people think that whenever a raise comes from the player on the button, the button always has a weak hand. If an opponent thinks you're trying to steal with a weak hand, he is likely to reraise you. You need to recognize which players have that mentality so that you can use it to your advantage. For example, when you catch pocket aces or another high pair on the button, you can raise knowing that your opponent(s) is probably going to reraise. His reraise then allows you to get maximum value from your good hand.

7. The Bluff Is an Important Weapon

In limit hold'em, bluffing can get you into a lot of trouble because you are usually going to get called. This is particularly true in low-limit games in which the pots are usually multiway. Often your limit hold'em opponents are correct in calling at the river, even if they suspect they may be beaten, because it costs only one additional bet to buy the chance of winning a pot that is giving them the correct pot odds. In no-limit hold'em, the bluff is an important strategic weapon that you can use to shut out an opponent who may have a better hand than yours. In Part Six we explain when and how to bluff. In Part Nine you will find bluffing practice hands.

8. Don't Despair When You Get Behind

In no-limit hold'em, it is far easier to "catch up" when you become short-chipped than it is in limit hold'em. If someone has two or three times your chips, all you have to do is go all in with him on one hand and you'll double up. Then you will be even or have more chips than your opponent. When a player has exactly a three-to-one advantage over you in chips, you're only two hands away from breaking him. You have to look at your whole stack as though it's one bet. That's why you don't push the panic button if you get outchipped by the opposition.

"When I won the World Series in 1991," Brad relates, "I was heads up at the championship table with Don Holt, who had about $2 million to my approximate $200,000. At that point all I was doing was looking for hands to double through with, and then double through again.

"Fortunately for me, I was able to double through to approximately $400,000, then to $800,000, and then to winning a 1.6 million pot on the last hand when I held the K♠ J♠ and flopped a pair of jacks for the win. So, don't give up when you are behind—spend your time looking for hands that you can double up with. Pretend that you are chopping down a tree with an axe—one chunk at a time—until it falls down."

PART FOUR

How to Determine the Strength of Your Hand

The First Winning Skill of No-Limit Texas Hold'em

Most likely, you will begin playing no-limit hold'em in a tournament or a one-table satellite. This is because—except for some very big on-land casino cash games and some small online casino cash games—no-limit hold'em is not usually spread as a cash game. It is primarily played as a tournament game, and it is the game that is most often played in the championship event of on-land and online tournaments.

To be a successful tournament player at any poker game, you must play a balancing act similar to a juggler who has seven balls in the air at one time. This chapter explains how to balance the critical factors in tournaments so that you can make it to the final table as often as possible and with as many chips as possible. The quality of your decisions depends on how well you integrate these seven factors into your game plan at every stage of the tournament.

The Seven Factors in the Balancing Act
- The strength of your hand
- The size of the blinds in relation to your stack
- How soon the limits are going to rise
- How many chips you have
- The size of your bet
- Your position at the table
- The playing style of your opponents

These seven factors are interrelated. That is, they work in unison with each other rather than in isolation. In some situations, your chip count will play a more important role in making a quality decision than the strength of your hand. In other scenarios, your table position plus the playing style of your opponent(s) will take precedence over your chip count.

No-limit hold'em is a game that requires judgment. You may decide to play a hand one way and then, after discussing it with a friend who is knowledgeable, find that he would have played it differently. Who is right? Neither of you is necessarily dead right or dead wrong. It all depends on how you and your friend balanced the way your opponents were playing, the amount of chips they had, how many chips you had, and the value of your hand in that particular situation.

The right way to play a hand is not set in stone—there is more than one way to play every hand. Understanding that, debating with other good players on the topic of how to play specific hands in certain situations can make you a better player. If you remain open minded enough to see both sides of the story, you can grow. Your differences of opinion usually occur because you and your poker buddies put more emphasis on one factor than the other. In essence, you are balancing things from different perspectives and that is why you see things in two different ways. We invite you to join in our discussions of no-limit hold'em by visiting *www.pokerbooks.com.*

Now let us talk in depth about the four major skills that you will need to master the balancing act and win at no-limit hold'em. They are:

> • Evaluating the Strength of Your Hand
> • Determining How Much to Bet
> • Understanding Your Opponents
> • Knowing When and How to Bluff

How to Determine the Strength of Your Hand

The first winning skill of no-limit Texas hold'em is evaluating the strength of your hand. The value of a hand is affected by these four factors:

> • Your Cards
> • Your Position at the Table
> • How Many Opponents You Have
> • The Playing Style of Your Opponents

It is difficult to discuss the strength of your hand without talking about your position at the table. When the other players have to act before you, you have a terrific advantage. Late position or having the button always gives you a much clearer idea of the relative strength of the hands that your opponents have, unless they have limped in with a big hand to try to trap you. When you are sitting up front, you aren't able to get any information on the value of your opponents' hands before you act. This is why you need greater card strength to enter the pot in the first three positions after the big blind. In essence, information is the name of the game.

Your Cards

Pictured on the next page are the hands that we suggest playing from a front position. Of course, you can play these strong hands from any position at the table.

With the big pairs—aces, kings, queens, jacks—you can bring it in for a normal raise of three to four times the size of the big blind. With all of the other pairs (tens and lower), you want to come in cheaply in the hope of hitting a set on the flop. You want to see the flop before putting any serious money into the pot. "No set, no bet" is the guideline.

When you have pocket aces or kings, it is preferable to get the money in before the flop. You may occasionally limp from up front with aces or kings in the hope that an opponent sitting behind you will raise, in which case you can reraise. By sometimes limping with the big pairs or suited connectors, your opponents might give you more respect in subsequent hands. In other words, they may not raise you on those occasions when you limp in with a small pair because they are fearful that you have a big pair, like they have seen you limp in with before.

Be very cautious with pocket queens and jacks because they are far more vulnerable than aces and kings. It is always possible that an opponent could have an overpair of kings or aces in the pocket or hit an ace or king on the flop to beat you.

Early Position Hands

Hand One

Hand Two

Hand Three

Hand Four

Hand Five

Hand Six

If you have a big pair, A-K or sometimes A-Q, you will usually play these hands from any position, depending on the action. In fact when you have aces or kings, it can be an advantage to act first. The reason for this is because, if you bring it in for a raise, a player in a later position may reraise you. This gives you the opportunity of raising again or just calling and trapping him after the flop. Most of the time, though, you prefer having position on your opponents, no matter your starting hand.

Playing in early positions, you simply have more players to act behind you. Anybody could pick up a hand and raise you, thus forcing you to fold—unless, of course, you have one of the premium hands, aces or kings. The way you play your hand can change dramatically, especially if you get short on chips, or if your opponents get short. Refer to the Betting Charts on pages 60-61.

Play middle position with caution, unless you have a premium pair, A-K, or A-Q. If you do decide to enter the pot with a somewhat marginal hand such as a small pair or suited connectors, you must be prepared to abandon ship if someone puts in any kind of substantial raise. That is why small pairs play much better in late position with several limpers already in the pot. You are trying to hit a flop and win a big pot on the cheap. Limping in from early position with these hands makes you a target for a raise, which you usually cannot call with a marginal hand.

Some of the hands that you might consider entering the pot with from middle position or later are pictured on the next page. If you are the first one to enter the pot, usually bring it in for a standard raise. In particular, this strategy applies to the middle and later stages of the tournament.

Middle Position Hands

Hand One

Hand Two

Hand Three

Hand Four

Hand Five

Hand Six

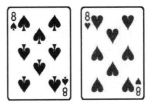

Late Position Hands

Hand One

Hand Two

Hand Three

Hand Four

Hand Five

Hand Six

Hand Seven — Any Low Pair

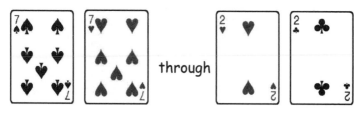

through

When you are sitting in late position, you also can enter the pot with some other hands, in addition to the hands that are pictured on the facing page. If the pot has not been raised, you can play any low pair from sevens to deuces. You also can play most suited connectors in unraised pots.

Whether you limp in late position, or bring it in for a raise, depends on what your opponents do before it is your turn to act. If you are the first one in the pot, you might bring it in for the standard raise. However if two or more limpers are already in the pot, you should only raise with a big pair or an A-K.

Your Position at the Table

Your table position is especially important in no-limit hold'em. Anytime you play a hand in no-limit hold'em, you could be putting your entire stack at risk. These are good reasons to select the hands that you play very carefully. Remember that the earlier you have to act, the stronger the hand you need. If you are an experienced limit hold'em player, the most important thing to remember in this section is that—until you get more mileage under your belt—you will not be playing as many hands in no-limit hold'em as you have been playing in limit hold'em. In other words, you must be more selective in no-limit hold'em.

Play more conservatively in early positions. Whenever you enter a pot from a front position, you are laying yourself open to raises and reraises from players who can act after you do. In the first three positions after the blind, you definitely want to play only premium hands and usually bring it in for a raise when you enter the pot. You can play more liberally from middle to late position in unraised pots when two or three limpers are in the pot. You are looking for a situation where you can win a pot and maybe double up, all the while trying to avoid getting eliminated. Always remember that you cannot win the tournament during the first round of play, but you can lose it if you make a mistake.

If you are last to act in no-limit tournaments you can often pick up the pot with a modest bet when it is checked to you. The legendary Doyle Brunson once said that he could beat any no-limit game without looking at his hole cards if he had last action and nobody knew he hadn't looked. This should give you an idea of just how important position is in all stages of a tournament.

How Many Opponents You Have

The relative strength of a starting hand changes depending on the number of players in the game. Because more people are playing against you when the game is 10-handed, you need a stronger starting hand than you would need when the game is five-handed, for example. A marginal hand that you would throw away when the game is 10-handed may become playable when the table is short. Also remember that when the game is 10-handed in the early stage of the tournament, there isn't much blind money in the pot to fight for, therefore you have less reason to try to steal pots with substandard hands.

Trouble hands can be even more trouble in no-limit hold'em than they are in limit hold'em. The blinds are very small in relation to the risks involved, so why get involved with a K-Q when someone raises in front of you? You could lose your whole stack with this trouble hand.

What kinds of hands do you raise with in the first round? If you're in early position, you want to have a big pair, A-K or possibly A-Q to bring it in for a raise. Be leery of raising with A-J – there's always the chance that someone behind you will reraise and you can't take a lot of heat with A-J. You might want to just limp in with A-J, but if you do raise with it, we suggest that you raise only three times the size of the big blind.

With A-K or A-Q, we also suggest raising three to four times the big blind. Then if one or two players call, you can take a stab at the pot on the flop to try to pick it up, if you hit or if you don't. If you hit the flop, you might check it and give someone behind you the opportunity to bet so that you can check-raise him. The check-raise is very strong in no-limit because you can win all of your opponent's chips at one time. So if you get a hand to trap them with, you can open the noose with a check and then tighten the noose with a check-raise when they bet.

We know that raising from up front with hands such as K-J or K-Q is shaky, but what about raising from middle to late position with these hands? In the early stage of the tournament, you usually do not raise with these trouble hands, even if nobody has entered the pot. Why? Because the blinds are so small that there's practically nothing in the pot to steal. And if you get played with by somebody who reraises behind you, he probably has a better hand than yours.

The only times that you might consider raising with one of these marginal hands are:

(1) A player with very few chips has limped into the pot in front of you, and

(2) The blinds are players who will give up their hands

easily. In any other circumstances, you need a premium hand in order to raise from middle to late position during the first round of play.

"In the first round I don't do a lot of raising," Brad says, "because with $10-$15 blinds there is only $25 in the pot." When you see someone limping in no-limit, especially if he's sitting in the first few seats, a warning light should flash in your mind. A limper can be dangerous. They can always be limping with a big hand. So you might just limp with the trouble hands if you want to play. Of course you don't really need to play them because the blinds are so low in the first level. You want a premium hand when you raise because there's very little to pick up anyway. The ratio of reward to risk favors the risk when the blinds are small.

"I'm just trying to manage the size of the pot," Brad says, "and I'm protecting my chips. I don't want to lose any chips because they're valuable." Your chips are your army and the fewer soldiers you have, the more valuable each one is.

PART FIVE

Determining How Much to Bet

The Second Winning Skill of No-Limit Texas Hold'em

Determining how much to bet is the second winning skill of no-limit Texas hold'em. These "Balancing Act" factors affect the size of your bet:

> • The Strength of Your Hand
> • The Number of Chips You Have
> • The Size of the Blinds
> • How Soon the Limit s Will Rise
> • The Nature of Your Opponents

What Is Your Betting Goal?

How much you bet depends on what you are trying to do. For example, your goal might be to eliminate players. If so, you might bet more than you ordinarily would. Another betting goal is to try to trap an opponent, in which case you might bet a little less. You also might want to try to represent a weak hand. Or you may try to steal the pot with a bluff bet.

Most players who are accustomed to playing limit hold'em do not choose the appropriate amount of chips to bet when they first start playing no-limit poker. They either underbet or overbet the pot. Many of them simply make a "mini-raise" that is double the amount of the big blind, the amount they are accustomed to raising in limit hold'em. Inexperienced players who make mini-raises don't realize that they could just call instead. There is hardly any difference between raising to two bets and just putting in one bet in no-limit hold'em. And some novices have just one move—all-in. We would like to give you a better idea of how much you should bet in no-limit hold'em so that when you raise, you will be confident that you are correct in your betting strategy.

Betting Guidelines

We like to bring it in for between three or four times the size of the big blind when we are the first one in the pot. But a lot of players make the mistake of gauging the size of their raise by the strength of their hand. In *Championship No-Limit & Pot-Limit Hold'em*, T.J. Cloutier and Tom McEvoy suggest that you always raise the same amount (three to four times the big blind) so that you won't give your opponents any clues about the strength of your cards.

Players tend to follow the leader. That is, it seems that if the first player who raises in the tournament overbets the pot by bringing it in for $100 when the blinds are $10-$15, it seems that everyone who raises after that follows suit by raising the same amount. "When that happens," Brad notes, "I usually ask out loud 'What's the minimum you can come in for?' I ask that question because if my opponents start raising too much, they stop me from being able to just call and thus force me to have a big hand to be able to play with them." You do not need to follow the leader—you can raise the amount of chips that you believe is correct, no matter what your opponents have been doing.

Overbetting the Pot

There are certain situations, however, when you can overbet the pot by a little bit. For example, suppose you get lucky in the first round and one of your opponents throws off all his chips to you. Now you have chips—and you need to protect them. You don't want to give anybody a shot at making two pair when you're holding pocket aces for a small amount of money, so you might overbet the pot a little bit.

For example, you might bring it in for six times the big blind rather than four times the big blind. Sometimes overbetting the pot works to your advantage in another way. One of your opponents might think, "He's betting too much, he's just trying to steal this pot." And he calls you when he shouldn't.

Over the past few years, it seems that players have started moving in all their chips more frequently. When a player moves all in, it often means that he is inexperienced or doesn't know how to bet. Of course there is a benefit to moving all in, namely that no one can outplay you. If someone calls, the decision is over with and you cannot make a mistake. You may have made a mistake by shoving all in to begin with, but you cannot make any further mistakes since you are going to the river. No matter what cards come on the flop, even if you made an error in betting, you could get lucky and draw out on your opponent.

The All-In Bet

The all-in move seems to be more prevalent in low-limit tournaments. Some people refer to it as the "one-bet mentality," because the only bet that some players seem to have is the all-or-nothing bet. We don't want our readers to think that the all-in bet is the best way to go—there is a time to go all in, and there is a time not to.

For example, moving all in can be an effective tactic when you believe that you're outclassed in the tournament. Maybe you're playing against a world-class player and you think you're at a skill disadvantage. In this case, even a top player cannot outplay you after the flop when you're all in, whereas he may be able to outplay you from the flop onward if you still have chips to play with. This is one reason why we have tried to take some of the decisions away from you in certain situations by limiting the number of hands that you play. After you get more experience at no-limit hold'em, you will be able to play another way.

There are other times, too, when you might consider going all-in rather than raising three to four times the size of the big blind. You can bet all-in, for example, when you have a medium to short stack. Your all-in bet lets your opponents know that you are going all the way to the river with your hand. You raise all-in because many inexperienced players do not understand when their opponents are fully committed to the pot, and their lack of knowledge can lead them to call your standard raise with a substandard holding and possibly put a bad beat on your better hand.

You might also raise all-in when you have a very big stack and you're playing against a short stack. You do it so that the short stack knows that he has to fully commit (put in all his chips) in order to call. Although you would be more likely to make this play from the fourth round onward when the blinds are hefty, you might actually make it during any stage of the tournament depending on your chip position.

Also look for the "all-in" mentality in some of your opponents, especially inexperienced players who have not read this book and, therefore, do not know how to bet their hands. If they have a hand they want to play, they will often overbet the pot by shoving in all their chips simply because they don't know the correct amount to bet. They are either afraid to play a pot or they don't know what else to do. Say it's the first level with $10-$15 blinds. You have a hand that you want to raise with. The normal raise would be $45 to $60, three to four times the big blind if you are the first one in the pot. A big raise would be $100, or about seven times the big blind.

One of the worst plays that we see novice players make in no-limit tournaments is making a small raise, such as double the big blind, after several people have limped in the pot. They are reopening the betting for players to reraise. This is absolutely mindless. Time and again we have seen an early limper come over the top of the small raise with a big reraise, causing everyone to fold, including the player who made the small raise. What does this type of raise accomplish? Usually, it results in more harm than good.

If the idea is to win the pot before the flop, that kind of raise would not eliminate anybody who already limped in. It will make the pot slightly bigger, but it will also encourage more gambling, if anything. If you have a premium hand such as a big pair, you want to eliminate players to increase your chances of winning, not encourage more of them to gamble with you—which is what you do when you make the pot slightly bigger with a small raise. So, if you have a good hand in late position, why not just see the flop for the minimum bet and decide what to do after the flop? You usually have position on most of the limpers in the pot, which also favors you.

Making the Minimum Raise

Sometimes you will see players make the minimum raise of double the size of the big blind when they are the first player in the pot. That is different. A player may be using deception to disguise the strength of his hand, or he may simply be mixing up his play. Raising the minimum bet should be done only when you are the first one in the pot, not after several limpers have come in.

Raising the minimum amount is one way to slow-play a hand. In no-limit hold'em, expect to see more players slow-play their hands trying to trap you. This happens because in limit hold'em, you can only make one extra bet by slow playing, whereas in no-limit hold'em, you can wipe out your opponent's whole stack in one pop.

How Many Chips You Have

Throughout the tournament the number of chips you have helps determine your strategy. Since the biggest payoffs in the tournament are the top three places, even the bigger stacks need to keep accumulating chips so they can reach one of those coveted positions.

Some players with a super-aggressive style will take a lot more chances to get a hold of chips early in the tournament. If the tournament allows unlimited rebuys for the first hour, these players will rebuy time and again until they win some pots and get some chips. They will gamble with the worst of it during the rebuy period and often beyond. Even though this is a viable strategy, it is an expensive one. Quite often super-aggressive "kamikazes" will crash and burn early in the tournament, especially if they don't slow down a bit after the rebuy period is over.

We recommend a more conservative approach. We suggest that you wait for better hands and try to pick off these very fast-action players. You need to be patient and recognize when you have an opportunity to strike. Knowing when those opportunities arise is part of the reason you bought this book—and we're here to teach you.

No matter what your chip count, you're almost always going to play big pairs, A-K and often A-Q. There are times to fold these hands, but for the most part, you are going to play them, at least before the flop. The bigger the blinds and the shorter your stack, the more likely you are to simply move in with these premium hands before the flop.

The bigger your stack, the more likely you are to put your opponent(s) all in before or on the flop with these same hands. The medium stacks have a more difficult decision to make. Sometimes it is okay to commit all your chips, but at other times you need to at least see the flop before doing so. This requires judgment.

Always keep in mind that the bigger the blinds, the more risk you and your opponents must take to stay alive. One of the main points in *Tournament Poker* is that you have to survive long enough to give yourself a chance to get lucky. And sometimes you just have to take a few more risks to survive.

The Size of the Blinds

Even though you're playing with small blinds in the early rounds, you can still get broke on the first hand you play, in contrast to limit hold'em where you are protected by the prescribed amount of the bets. In no-limit hold'em, you can move in your whole stack at any time, no matter how small the blinds are. A lot of times you'll see several players go out during the first level of play, which virtually never happens in limit hold'em tournaments.

In the early stages of no-limit hold'em tournaments, you have far less reason to attack the blinds without a premium hand because the reward of picking up the blinds is not worth the risk of losing a lot of chips. This especially applies to tournaments that have no rebuys. If you are in a small tournament with multiple rebuys and are prepared to rebuy when needed, then it is okay to take a few more risks and mix it up a little more to try to win some bigger pots and accumulate chips. Once the rebuy period is over—which usually lasts for about an hour, sometimes a little longer—the tournament starts in earnest. By then the blinds are higher and there is more money in the pot to go after.

Also, many no-limit tournaments start having an ante in addition to the blinds around the fifth or sixth level of play. When that happens, just sitting on your stack and playing very conservatively will cause your stack to start shrinking, thus eroding your chip position. Therefore you need to take a few more calculated risks to maintain and improve your chip position. Naturally, in the latter stages of the tournament the blinds and antes get quite large and people start moving in more and more. They don't always have premium hands when this happens.

How Soon the Limits Are Going to Rise

The rate the blinds go up is more of a factor in the middle stages and later stages of the tournament than it is in the early rounds. The further you are into the tournament, the timing of increases in the blinds and antes becomes more important. If you have a large stack of chips, the bigger blinds are less important. It is the medium and short stacks that are in greater danger from the ever-increasing blinds. When you realize that the limits are going to rise before you can take the blinds at their current, smaller amounts—you know that you will have to go through higher blinds in a very short time—your strategy may be affected.

For example, you might play a marginal hand like K-J before the blind gets to you just because it figures to be better than a random blind hand. Remember that everyone, including the big stacks, is always fighting the clock.

A similar thing happens in football games. The team with the lead is trying to protect that lead while the team that is trailing has to take more chances to catch up. That is what the big and little stacks are trying to do. The big stacks want to protect their chip position, while the medium and small stacks want to catch up. All this is going on while the clock is ticking and the blinds and antes are continually increasing until the tournament is over. The big stacks also want to increase their chips just as football teams want to increase their lead. When the gun goes off in a football game, the team with the lead is declared the winner. In poker the winner is declared only when one person has won all the chips. Thankfully, there are usually several money payoffs in poker rather than just one winner, as there is in football.

On the following pages, you will find a Betting Chart that we have prepared especially as a betting guide for new no-limit Texas hold'em players. We hope that it helps you become a winning player.

Reading the Betting Chart

To determine how much you should raise when you have an average (or above) number of chips, simply note what round you are in, the size of the blinds, and the amount of a normal raise. Using these numbers, you will have a very good idea of how much to bet. If antes are required, refer to the "With Antes" chart. If they aren't, use the "No Antes" chart. If your chip count has fallen into the "Trouble Stack" category or has dropped into the "Move-In" zone, use those numbers to determine how much you should bet.

The "ante" column in this chart is typical of the ante structure used by most online casinos. In on-land casinos, the ante structure is usually higher. When you want to make a normal raise *after* the antes have come into play, it is acceptable to raise up to five times the size of the big blind *if* you are the first player in the pot.

No-Limit Hold'em Betting Chart
With No Antes

Round	Small Blind	Big Blind	Normal Raise	Trouble Stack	Move-In Stack
1	5	10	30-40	150	50
2	10	20	60-80	200	100
3	15	30	90-120	300	150
4	25	50	150-200	500	250
5	50	100	300-400	1000	500
6	75	150	450-600	1500	750
7	100	200	600-800	2000	1000
8	150	300	900-1200	3000	1500
9	200	400	1200-1600	4000	2000
10	300	600	1800-2400	4800	3000
11	400	800	2400-3200	6400	4000
12	600	1200	3600-4800	9600	6000
13	1000	2000	6000-8000	14000	8000
14	1500	3000	9000-12000	21000	12000
15	2000	4000	12000-16000	28000	16000
16	3000	6000	18000-24000	42000	24000

No-Limit Hold'em Betting Chart
With Antes

Round	Small Blind	Big Blind	Ante	Normal Raise	Trouble Stack	Move-In Stack
1	5	10	0	30-40	150	50
2	10	20	0	60-80	200	100
3	15	30	0	90-120	300	150
4	25	50	0	150-200	500	250
5	50	100	0	300-400	1000	500
6	75	150	0	450-600	1500	750
7	100	200	0	600-800	2000	1000
8	100	200	25	600-1000	2600	1600
	150	300	25	900-1200	3400	2000
9	200	400	25	1200-2000	4200	2500
10	300	600	50	1800-3000	5400	3400
11	400	800	50	2400-4000	6600	4200
12	600	1200	75	3600-6000	9900	6200
13	1000	2000	100	6000-10000	15600	9800
14	1500	3000	150	9000-15000	23400	14700
15	2000	4000	200	12000-20000	31200	19500
16	3000	6000	300	18000-30000	46800	30000

The Normal Raise Column

Your stack is in the normal range when your chip count is higher than the chip counts in the trouble stack and move-in stack columns. This is in relation to the blinds and antes in effect during that particular round.

Your normal raise should be three to four times the size of the big blind. Hands that we suggest making a normal raise with include A-A, K-K, Q-Q, A-K, J-J, and A-Q during any round of the tournament from any position of the table if we are first to come into the pot.

If you are in late position you can make the normal raise with smaller pairs, A-J, K-Q, or even J-10 when there are players in the blinds that you think might fold against your raise.

The Trouble Stack Column

When your stack of chips has dropped to the amount listed in the Trouble Zone—but it has not fallen into the Move-In Zone—you have the option of making "normal" raises (three to four times the big blind) all the way up to all-in moves.

The higher the blinds and antes, the more we lean toward moving all in because just winning the blinds and antes will help your chip position. However, if you have a hand that you want action with—a pair of aces or kings, for example—you might want to raise three times the big blind rather than moving all-in. You are hoping to get callers and win a big pot. Being able to play a short stack effectively will help your chances tremendously.

The Move-In Stack Column

When your chips have sunk into the Move-In Zone, you are in big trouble—you're in jeopardy of bombing out of the tournament. You must make a move to try get more chips or you will go broke. When you fall into the Move-In Zone, you have to try to pick up the blinds at least once a round.

Whenever you come into the pot, you are moving all in. If you don't catch one of the better hands, you may have to simply attack any player in the big blind that you think will fold. When you move in with a weak hand trying to pick up the pot, you are betting that no one has a hand that they can call with. This is when reading your opponents, knowing who is most likely to fold, is very important.

When your chips have dipped into the Move-In Zone, it is much better to fire and take a chance with a weaker hand than to just sit back and let the blinds and antes destroy your stack. Your opponents know that just going through the blinds will demolish your stack; therefore they tend to call you with mediocre hands if they think that you're making a move at the pot. If you go broke firing in your stack just trying to stay alive, don't feel embarrassed—at least you tried to change your miserable chip position.

Hands that Tom and I like to play when we move in include the premium hands, of course, plus suited connectors such as 6♠ 5♠, 7♣ 6♣, 8♦ 7♦, 9♥ 8♥, 10♠ 9♠, or J♠ 10♠. You can also move in with any pair, any two face cards, and any hand that contains an ace. As long as you don't run into an overpair or someone holding one of your cards, you are not that big of a dog with your hand if you do get called. Remember that you want to be the first one in the pot with these marginal hands, not a caller. You can call, of course, if you have a premium hand.

PART SIX

Understanding Your Opponents

The Third Winning Skill of No-Limit Texas Hold'em

Understanding your opponents is the third winning skill of no-limit hold'em. Your game strategy will often be affected by the types of players you are playing against. This is particularly true in no-limit hold'em, where knowing the playing tendencies of your opponents is very important. We have identified a few classic types of players in this part and have given them names. This will help you recognize them in the scenarios we discuss in later sections of this book.

Action Al raises a lot of pots. When he has the opportunity to act after you do, you can usually count on him to call or raise. You've noticed, though, that he often (but not always) shows down good cards. *Reckless Rick* is in overdrive. He raises too often, usually without any logical reason, often overbets the pot, and has shown some weak hands. He's usually willing to go to war with Action Al. *Passive Paul* just calls, even when he has a premium hand. He seems afraid to get into the battle.

Novice Nancy is experimenting with no-limit play after years of playing limit hold'em. She usually either overbets or underbets the pot, and sometimes calls when she shouldn't. *Tight Ted* has cobwebs on his chips. When he raises, you know that he has a premium hand. *Loose Louie* is on a roll and has held cards over you several times. He plays a lot of hands, including middle connectors and small pairs.

Solid Sam is aggressive when he plays a hand, but always seems to select the right situations and turns over strong cards at the showdown. *Authority Artie* is the resident critic at the table. He always has something to say about the way you play your hands. He can embarrass you by criticizing your play and lead you to feel very uncomfortable.

These types of players are very typical of the players you will actually be competing against in no-limit poker tournaments. Now let's look at some tips on how to play against each of the eight players we have profiled.

How to Play Against Different Types of Opponents

Action Al and Reckless Rick are "rammer-jammers"—they raise and reraise way more than they should. Both can be very dangerous when they catch some cards. They give so much loose action that you are often forced to give them action with less than the nuts, because they will both try to run over you. Action Al is more dangerous than Reckless Rick, because he knows how to play when he gets good cards or a good flop. Al will show you a good hand more often than Rick.

Reckless Rick's style might be better defined by calling him a maniac. Maniacs are the most difficult players to play against because it is very hard to put them on a specific hand. You will usually have to show a maniac the best hand. The maniac is the easiest person to trap when you do have the goods, but if you're catching only marginal cards, he can bluff you or force you to take a stand when you don't want to.

Most of the time, a maniac like Rick will crash and burn early. If he gets a hold of some chips, however, you will just have to be patient and wait for the opportunity to trap him with a better hand. Playing like a maniac isn't all bad. Sometimes a Reckless Rick will win a tournament because his aggressive style allows him to win many uncontested pots, substantially increasing his chances of winning the tournament.

Passive Paul is far easier to play against than Al or Rick. He will call if he has anything, but he will seldom bet and get full value out of his premium hands. If we bet and Paul calls us after the flop, we know he has hit something, if only a draw. We can bet into Paul with good hands, but we must be leery of bluffing him if he has called on the flop. If Passive Paul comes out betting or check-raises us, we know he has a real hand, and we must act with caution. We should continue playing only with strong hands ourselves.

Novice Nancy is more unpredictable than Passive Paul. Nancy usually cannot determine the relative strength of her hand after the flop and, therefore, is prone to making mistakes. By overbetting her strong hands, she "tells" us that we should avoid playing against her unless we have a strong hand. Nancy also underbets a lot of her hands, thus not protecting them from being drawn out on. Perhaps her biggest weakness is calling when she should fold. It is somewhat risky to try to bluff Novice Nancy, because she is a calling station. However, we can value bet some of our medium-strength hands because she will call us with something less. Nancy is the type of player we welcome to the game because she will find a way to give away her chips even when she has a big stack.

Tight Ted is by far the most predictable player at the table. You always know where he is at. You can run over his blinds, bluff him after the flop, and duck him when he bets. Ted does well against players like Action Al, Reckless Rick and Novice Nancy, who make lots of mistakes. That is, assuming that Ted doesn't go broke waiting to find a premium hand to play against them. Even Rick and Al know enough to be careful when Ted is in the pot betting into them.

Loose Louie is another player whose style is difficult to play against. Louie plays more hands than he should, even in raised pots, but he knows how to get value from his hands when he hits the flop. Because he plays so many hands he is often difficult to read. If you have a big pair and middle cards come on the flop, be careful—Louie might have hit the flop. If he is willing to give you a lot of action or moves in on you, be careful. Louie's style will often cause him to get shortstacked or broke early in the tournament, but if he hits a few hands, he can be dangerous. Often, however, he will continue to gamble with marginal hands, even with a big stack, and thus put himself in jeopardy of getting crippled or going broke later in the tournament. If he slows down with a big stack and doesn't gamble too much, he is capable of winning the tournament.

Solid Sam is not as conservative as Tight Ted, but he is easier to read than Al, Rick or Louie. He is a dangerous player who knows "where he is" (he understands the relative strength of his hand) at all times. He plays his position well, knows how to trap, and seldom gets out of line. When he is in the pot, especially if he comes in from early position, play cautiously against him. If he brings it in for a raise, you know that he has a solid hand—after all, his name is Solid Sam.

Being able to read Sam and being able to beat Sam are two different things. Sam's biggest problem in tournaments is that he might not get enough decent starting hands to play before the blinds and antes cause him to get shortstacked. He is not willing to take the same gambles that Al, Rick and Louie take. Sam usually lasts a long time, but often stays short-chipped and goes broke in the later rounds.

Authority Artie usually knows a lot less about the game than he thinks he does. Sometimes he will make a great play, such as snapping off a bluff when he has a weak hand. Other times he will fold a fairly strong hand when he shouldn't. He always knows when you make a bad play, but seldom knows when he makes a bad play. Artie is usually so busy talking and instructing that he misses the more subtle things going on around him. He is not dumb, just egotistical. Artie wins once in awhile, but usually fails in the clutch.

Classic Opponent Types
Tip Sheet

Action Al - Aggressive, raises a lot of pots but is a good player. Dangerous with good cards but plays too many hands

Reckless Rick - Raises too often, usually without logical reason, often overbets the pot, and has shown some weak hands. A "maniac" - difficult to play against, but easy to trap.

Passive Paul - Will call if he has any type of hand, and seldom will bet, even with premium hands. He seems afraid to get into the battle.

Novice Nancy - Usually overbets or underbets the pot and sometimes calls when she should fold. Makes many mistakes.

Tight Ted - When he raises, you know that he has a premium hand. Very predictable.

Loose Louie - He plays a lot of hands—too many— including middle connectors and small pairs, and thus difficult to read. Plays good hands well. A real gambler.

Solid Sam - Aggressive when he plays a hand, but in the right situations; turns over strong cards at the showdown. A good, solid player.

Authority Artie - The resident critic who always has something to say about the way you play your hands. Makes some good plays, but some bad ones as well.

PART SEVEN

Knowing When and How to Bluff

The Fourth Winning Skill of No-Limit Texas Hold'em

Knowing when and how to bluff is the fourth winning skill of no-limit Texas hold'em. Pulling off a successful bluff is one of the most pleasurable aspects of playing poker. There's nothing quite like the satisfaction you get when you have caused your opponent(s) to lay down a better hand than yours. Some players would actually rather win with a bluff than with a legitimate hand! The intense feeling of satisfaction and superiority they get from bluffing successfully is the reason why.

It's hard to hold enough premium hands to win a tournament without doing some bluffing along the way. In tournaments the blinds keep getting higher and higher as time goes by and when you become short on chips, you eventually have to play some kind of hand just to stay in action. Naturally everyone wants to look down and find pocket aces, but sometimes—most of the time, in fact— they don't come our way. That is why we have to become creative just to stay alive so that we don't completely blind and ante our chips away.

Many factors enter the picture when you make the decision to risk your chips with what you consider to be a weak hand, one that you think wouldn't win in a show-down. In other words, you have to think of lots of things when you decide to bluff.

We have decided to write this part of the book in a question and answer format. Here are our answers to the questions that students most frequently ask us about bluffing.

What is bluffing?

Bluffing is betting with a hand that doesn't figure to be the best hand. Some people refer to it as betting "without a hand." You think that you can make your opponent(s) fold a better hand than yours so that you can win the pot even though you don't have the best hand. In this section, we discuss five types of bluffs—the semi-bluff, the steal bluff, the re-steal bluff, the follow-up bluff, and the total bluff.

What does "without a hand" mean?

Betting "without a hand" means betting without what you perceive to be the best hand. For example, suppose that you don't have a pair, but you do have a flush draw on the flop. Alas, you miss it at the river. You can't even beat an ace-high hand, but you think that your opponent is weak. You've put a good read on him and you bet with nothing. "To me, one of the biggest pleasures in poker," Brad says, "is making a big bet at somebody and seeing him throw away a better hand than you have. You just win it with guts."

Of course the bluff is much more effective in no-limit poker where you can make a big enough bet to get your opponents to fold better hands. In limit hold'em, it only costs an opponent one extra betting unit to call and if the pot is big enough, he will be correct in calling. For that reason, bluffing is not as effective in limit hold'em as it is in no-limit hold'em.

When do you bluff?

You usually bluff on the flop when you think your opponent is weak and you believe that a bet will win the pot for you—usually when you have position on your opponent and he has shown weakness by checking to you.

Another time you might bluff is when winning the pot increases your chances of winning the tournament so much that it justifies trying to pull off a bluff. If you lose the pot, it will knock you out of the tournament, but that's a chance that you must take. In cases like this, you might risk all of your chips with a bluff bet to try to pick up the pot.

What types of opponents are the easiest to bluff?

Being able to read your opponents correctly—knowing their playing styles—is the major factor in deciding who and when to bluff. You're looking for the type of opponents who are most likely to fold their hands—those who play very tight and the ones who are afraid of going broke. You don't want to bluff against Loose Louie, who will call with all sorts of marginal hands that could be slightly better than the hand you're bluff-betting with. You are more likely to be able to bluff players like Solid Sam or Tight Ted, who will fold marginal hands.

What question should you ask yourself before you bluff?

Here is a good question to ask yourself before you bet: "If I bet a large amount, what kind of hand would my opponent need to call my bet?" Would he need to have kings or aces? In other words, what are his criteria for calling big bets? He may not call a bet unless he has top pair with a good kicker on a flop such as K-10-6. But if the flop comes with small cards, 7-4-2 for example, an opponent may have a tough time calling a bet with a hand such as A-K or A-Q. Will he call with two overcards to the flop? A straight draw?

If you are observant enough, you can often limit the types of hands with which an opponent will call a bet. You can then answer your own question with, "If they don't have at least this type of hand, they're going to fold." Knowing the calling requirements of your opponents is important in making a successful, legitimate bet as well as a bluff-bet.

How much money should you bluff?

Usually you bluff an amount that is equal to the size of the pot. When you bluff that many chips, it usually means that your opponent will have to put in a substantial number of chips to call you. On televised tournaments you might see a player push all his chips into the pot. You might do this too if you are somewhat shortstacked. Say that the pot has $4,000 in it and your total stack is $6,000. If you're going to bluff, you may as well fire in all your chips. That way, nobody can reraise you. But say that the pot has $4,000 in it and you have $20,000 in chips. In this case, you might fire $4,000 at the pot, a pot-sized bet.

What is semi-bluffing?

Semi-bluffing is another play you'll see the players make at the championship table on television. The semi-bluff means that you put in chips with no pair, no nothing, when you probably have the worst hand—but you have some sort of a draw that gives you a chance to win the pot on a later street. You have a draw to a good hand, and you're taking the chance that your opponents will fold if you bet.

For example, suppose you have the A♦ K♦ and the flop comes with three little cards such as 7♦ 4♦ 2♣. Someone bets on the flop and you think that he probably has a pair or, possibly, an overpair to the flop. Your opponent may have a hand such as 9-9 or 10-10, or it is possible that he doesn't have a hand either. Whether or not he has a hand, you have outs—you have two overcards plus a flush draw. This is a hand that you have decided to go with, so you put in a big raise when he bets. That way you have a chance to win the pot right then and there if he is weak.

Now, suppose he checks to you. Even if you think he may have a pair, you might make a good-sized bet. He may very well fold his pair and you can win the pot un-contested. Even if you get called, you have outs to the hand—you could make the flush or hit one of your over-cards to win the pot. You also might make this play when you only have two overcards with no additional draw.

How can you steal the antes and blinds before the flop by bluffing?

The primary purpose of bluffing before the flop is to steal the blinds. When you try a steal bluff, you make a positional raise, sometimes with a marginal hand. As the blinds go up, you try to steal the blinds here and there just to keep going.

You usually make the bluff bet from late middle to late position when you are the first one in the pot. This means that you bet from three positions in front of the button through the button. The earlier you make a pre-flop raise to try to steal the blinds and antes, the riskier it is. If someone has already entered the pot, you usually do not consider trying to pull off an ante steal.

In the televised poker tournaments, you will notice that players often try to steal the antes and blinds with positional raises. At the final table of these big tournaments, the blinds are very high. Because of that, you will see players bluff-bet with just about any two cards, even 10-4 for example, to try to pick up the antes and blinds because it is so important in the very late stage of the tournament. Players will start to attack opponents that they believe will throw away their hands against a big raise.

Since you can see the players' hole cards, it's fun to watch someone with a hand like 9-2 make a big bet trying to steal the blinds. You can watch his opponent, who is usually in one of the blinds, carefully studying whether to call the raise with a marginal hand such as K-Q or K-J and finally deciding to fold. All the while, you're smiling because you know what he doesn't know—the raiser has nothing!

What is the resteal bluff?

Another type of bluff is the resteal. You think that an opponent is out of line and you go over the top (reraise) of him trying to pick up the pot. You are representing a strong hand by reraising. For example, say that somebody comes out with a bet and you think, "This guy is trying to steal the pot, so I'm going to try to resteal it from him." With that goal in mind, you reraise the pot with absolutely nothing. This is an advanced play that you frequently see at the championship tables of the televised World Poker Tour and the World Series of Poker.

What is the follow-up bluff?

It takes a lot of heart to bluff once and follow it with another bluff. Sometimes it works and wins a lot of chips, and other times it's a disaster. Suppose a player bluffs before the flop trying to pick up the blinds and antes and an opponent calls him. Now let's say that he misses the flop entirely. "I'll bluff some more," he thinks, "because I've got all those chips in the pot and I don't want to lose them. Maybe I can save them by firing in another bet." If the player who called the bluffer's pre-flop raise is first to act and he checks on the flop, it is almost automatic that the raiser will bet. The pre-flop caller will probably fold if he missed the flop and the raiser will win the hand with his follow-up bluff.

Here is an example of the danger in trying a follow-up bluff. Suppose the caller has a good hand. He is pretty sure that if he checks to you, you are going to bet. Therefore he can use position to his advantage and check his good hand to allow you, the raiser, to bet and thus set up a check-raise to win more chips. Say that he has two jacks and he called the pre-flop raise. The flop comes 7-4-2. He checks to you, believing that you are going to bluff at the pot. If you bet, he can reraise you and win the extra chips that you bet on the flop.

The follow-up bluff is a play that newcomers should be very cautious about trying. It requires a high level of skill to determine who and when you should try it against.

What is the total bluff?

The total bluff is similar to the steal bluff with one major exception. In the steal bluff, you might have a hand that is marginal but has some potential for winning. Examples include 8-7 suited, K-10 offsuit, or A-5 offsuit. In the total bluff, you have absolute trash in your hand— 7-2, 8-3, or 9-4, for example. You are gambling that nobody will call if you raise. The total bluff is usually attempted in late position when no one has entered the pot and the blinds are tight players who fold most marginal hands.

Suppose your chip stack has dwindled to the "move-in" size. (Refer to the "Move-In" column in the Betting Chart.) You have identified which player is the best candidate for you to attack with all your chips. You raise all in to try to win the blinds and antes—and you do it with any two cards. If your bluff works, you will win the blinds and antes, or you might draw out on your opponent if he calls. If it doesn't work, you will be rewarded with early retirement from the tournament.

After the flop, who normally does the bluffing?

It depends. In an unraised pot, it is often the first person who bets after the flop, usually because he thinks the flop missed everybody else. If the pot was raised before the flop, the player who is more apt to bluff after the flop is the raiser, since people are accustomed to routinely checking to the pre-flop raiser. He may have a legitimate hand, of course, but he runs the risk of getting trapped by an opponent who check-raises him, as some players check a big hand from up front when they are fairly sure that the pre-flop raiser will bet.

What type of pressure do you put on opponents when you bluff?

Getting broke or damaging their stack creates tremendous pressure on tournament players. Always remember that you—and your opponents—need a better hand to call a raise with than you need to bet with. If your opponents are short-chipped and they know that they're going to have to commit most of their chips, it will be more difficult for them to call without a "made" hand. You're putting pressure on them with your bet because they face the danger of going broke or crippling their stack if they call with a marginal hand. Nobody wants to get up and walk!

Suppose the tournament will be paying the top 18 spots and the action is down to 19 players. When it gets that close to a payday, players feel a lot of pressure if they must make a decision as to whether to call a raise with their case chips (the last chips they have in front of them). Going broke one spot out of the money is called finishing "on the bubble."

Or as Brad so eloquently puts it, "You hit the skunk hole!"

How do the changes in today's fast-action no-limit hold'em games affect your ability to bluff?

Today there are a lot more "action" players who are not playing "by the book" than there were in the past. And there are many more very aggressive players who are constantly on the attack. In the old days, many of the top players would never call a big raise with a hand as weak as an A-Q. In today's games, many players might call you with a hand as weak as an A-10. Some new players think that hands like A-Q, A-J or A-10 are big hands and they will call big raises with them, even occasionally reraising with them. This tendency is pertinent to bluffing because you should know that in today's tournaments, many players will call you with weaker hands that you would have expected them to call you with in the past.

What is one of the biggest bluffs you've ever seen in a tournament?

"I remember the biggest bluff you ever made, Tom, and it turned out to be the best bluff," Brad reminisced. "It happened at the Hall of Fame $5,000 championship no-limit hold'em event. We were down to twelve players, and guess who you bluffed? Me! And do you know what I had? The top set: kings. And guess what you caught? A flush. You bluffed on the flop and got there with the hand."

"That's true," Tom answered. "Sometimes you make the wrong move at the right time and then get lucky."

"I remember the first time I ever bluffed," Brad recalled. "I was 21 years old, playing in a no-limit lowball draw game. I had about $600 in front of me. My opponent and I got about $300 apiece in the pot before the draw. I take one card—now I'm looking down at a pair of sixes. I know that I can't win the pot unless I bluff at it. I was the first one to act, so I just moved in on him. I wanted that pot because all the money I had in the world was in it. He stalled and stalled and I could feel my stomach turning inside out so badly that I thought it was going to come out my throat. But I didn't move a muscle. Finally he folded. He had stood pat before the draw, so I knew that he definitely had me beaten. If he had called, I would have gone broke."

During the 1984 World Series of Poker, Cowboy Wolford pulled off what many consider to be the biggest bluff in WSOP history when he bluffed Jesse Alto at the championship table. In three-handed action with eventual winner Jack Keller, Wolford confronted Alto in a big pot. In the small blind, Keller folded before the flop when Alto bet on the button. Wolford called from the big blind. The flop came A♣ K♦ 9♣. Wolford bet $15,000 and Alto called. The turn card was the K♥. Wolford fired another $40,000 at the pot. Again Alto called.

When the 2♠ came at the river, Wolford pushed his last $101,000 into the middle. Alto thought about it at length and finally folded. That's when, according to reporter Bobby Baldwin, "The cowboy exercised a psychological option in choosing to show his nothing-but-nerve cards." The Texas calf-roping champion had bluffed Alto, one of the famous old-time road gamblers, with the 5♠ 4♣. The two men had gambled together on the Texas poker circuit for years, so Wolford knew Alto's style of play and apparently used that knowledge to his advantage in this classic example of the follow-up bluff.

The legendary Byron "Cowboy" Wolford at the 1979 World Series of Poker. Five years later in 1984 the Texas road gambler placed second to Jack Keller in the championship event after pulling off the most famous bluff in World Series of Poker history. Wolford chronicled his poker and rodeo adventures in his 2000 book (written with Dana Smith), *Cowboys, Gamblers & Hustlers*. He was 72 years old when he died in 2003, still playing poker for a living.

PART EIGHT

Tournament Practice Hands

How to Select, Bet & Play the Best Hands

Before you begin studying the tournament practice hands we give you in this section, try to forget many of the fancy plays you've seen top players make on national television. Most of the opponents you will be playing against in low-limit, beginner tournaments are playing at your same level of expertise. This means that they will not understand many of the more advanced moves that world-class players sometimes make. In other words, most beginners at no-limit hold'em are far more likely to simply call you down than they are to fold in response to a fancy play.

After you have learned the basic principles of no-limit hold'em tournament play and have gained enough experience to move up the ladder of knowledge, you can expand your range of moves to include more sophisticated plays. But for now, let's keep it simple.

As beginning no-limit hold'em players, we are going to play a limited number of premium hands. As your ability improves you will be able to start branching out from these hands and play a few additional ones. We recommend that you play only these hands until your skill has improved to a point where you have a very good idea of what is going on. By that we mean that you understand the value of your starting hands very well, and whether the flop is good or bad for your hand. You also need to be good at reading your opponents before you step up to more advanced strategies.

Because we give you a strict selection of hands that you will be playing, you will have plenty of time between your playable hands to practice various things. We want you to be very observant of everything that's going on in the game. By being observant you will spot things that will help you read your opponents better and thus make better decisions.

When you are not in a hand, ask yourself the following questions. Your answers will help you improve your reading ability when you are playing a hand.

- How often do they come into the pot?
- In what position do they raise?
- What kind of hands do they have when they raise?
- Do they raise a lot?
- How much do they raise with various types of hands?
- What kind of hands do they limp with?
- What cards are they showing down?
- How does it affect their mood when they lose?
- How does it affect their mood when they win a hand?
- Can you see any patterns in their play?

By being very observant and asking yourself all these questions, you should be able to form a very good idea as to the kinds of hands your opponents are playing. When you get in tune, you will probably amaze yourself with how accurate your reads have become.

Answering these questions is an exercise that you can do even when you are a spectator of a game that is being played on television, in an on-land casino, or in an Internet casino. It's a great way to learn to read players.

Remember that you will be playing with opponents who have different playing styles. Your strategy will often be affected by the type of players you are playing against. In the following tournament scenarios, we use the player types listed earlier in this book.

Here's a quick review:

1) *Action Al* raises a lot of pots. When he has the opportunity to act after you do, you can usually count on him to reraise. You've noticed, though, that he often (but not always) shows down good cards.

2) *Reckless Rick* is in overdrive. He raises too often, usually without any logical reason, often overbets the pot, and has shown some weak hands. He's usually willing to go to war with Action Al.

3) *Passive Paul* just calls, even when he has a premium hand. He seems afraid to get into the battle.

4) *Novice Nancy* is experimenting with no-limit play after years of playing limit hold'em. She usually either overbets or underbets the pot, and sometimes calls when she shouldn't.

5) *Tight Ted* has cobwebs on his chips. When he raises, you know that he has a premium hand.

6) *Loose Louie* is on a roll and has held cards over

you several times. He plays a lot of hands, including middle connectors and small pairs.

7) *Solid Sam* is aggressive when he plays a hand, but always seems to select the right situations and turns over strong cards at the showdown.

8) *Authority Artie* is the resident critic at the table. He always has something negative to say about the way you play your hands, and his comments can be quite embarrassing. Artie also knows the rules of every card game ever invented.

We use these players' names as shortcuts to describe the types of opponents you will be facing before the flop in each of the following tournament scenarios.

The Tournament Structure

You are playing a no-limit hold'em tournament. Each player starts with $1,000 in tournament chips. Each round lasts 30 minutes. The blinds in Round One are $10-$15. They increase to $10-$25 in Round Two and then go up to $25-$50 in Round Three. In Round Four the blinds increase to $50-$100. Round Five blinds are $75-$150. In Round Six they increase to $100-$200 and continue to increase in each round through the end of the tournament.

Your Tournament Strategy

You have decided to play conservatively in the early rounds of the tournament, being careful to select only premium hands to play. You will raise three to four times the size of the big blind when you play a hand and are the first player to enter the pot. If you decide to reraise, you will base the amount of chips you reraise on the situation.

Your criteria for reraising include the type of player who raised in front of you, what other players have done in answer to his initial raise, the types of players who can act after you, and the amount of chips you have in front of you.

You have prepared yourself for battle both mentally and emotionally. You intend to remain alert and observant to everything going on at your table at all times. You have brought your A-game to the tournament with you. Now let's shuffle up and deal!

Playing Big Pairs: Aces

How to Play Aces Before the Flop

Pocket aces is our favorite hand to start with. With A-A we normally want to raise three to four times the size of the big blind when we are the first player to enter the pot. You have the nuts before the flop and you hope someone reraises so that you will have the opportunity to raise again. With aces we would prefer getting all the money in before the flop. In fact when we are holding pocket aces, we would love to hear an opponent announce, "All in!"

Aces are very hard to lay down after the flop, so we try to get as many chips in the pot as possible before the flop. But caution—don't bet so much that you blow everyone out. You want action with aces—and that is why we recommend that you bring it in for three to four times the size of the big blind.

If someone has limped in front of you, just add what they brought it in for plus three to four times the size of the big blind. For example, suppose the blinds are $10-$25 and one person has limped. You bring it in for $100-$125. If two people have limped in, you would bring it in for $125-$150.

Now suppose an opponent raises the pot in front of you. What should you do? You should reraise at least double the amount he brought it in for. For example, with $10-$25 blinds, suppose your opponent raises to $100. You will normally raise to around $250, once again hoping that you get reraised.

Remember that with aces we want to get the maximum number of chips in the middle before the flop. We are always willing to put them all in before the flop. Aces will win approximately 81 percent of the time against another pair. That is a great edge to have over any other starting hand. Suppose you have aces against two opponents. One of them holds Q-Q and the other one has K-K. Your aces should win a little over 66 percent of the time.

Slow-Playing Aces

There are times when you might even want to slow-play with aces. Limping is one way to slow-play a big hand. You can limp (just call) when you think that someone will raise if you just limp into the pot. Another way that you can slow-play is by checking on the flop when you feel certain that an aggressive player cannot restrain himself from betting when you check.

The idea is to figure out the best way to get as much money as possible into the pot, which you expect to win. Sometimes slow-playing is the only way to do that because if you bet, you are pretty sure that your opponents will fold their hands. Your check on the flop may allow them to catch up and possibly give you some action on your premium hand. Of course when you slow-play a big hand, you take the risk of getting out-flopped. You are simply gambling that no one will get lucky against you.

Now let's have some fun with an "edutainment" feature of this book—multiple choice questions designed to help you think your way through strategic tournament situations.

SCENARIO 1

Suppose all the players have $1,000 in chips with the blinds at $10 and $25. You're sitting in first position. Looking down at your hole cards, you're thrilled to find:

How much should you open the pot for?

A. Open for $75-$100. This is the "normal" size of raise when the blinds are $10-$25. You are hoping that someone will reraise so that you can get all in before the flop.

B. Call the minimum $25 big blind in the hope that several players will limp behind you, followed by a raiser who raises to $100, for example. If this happens, you can reraise them to possibly get a lot of chips in before the flop.

Analysis

Both A and B are the correct plays. We recommend that you play the strategy in Example A when you first start out because it is "safer" and will help keep you out of trouble. We would rather see you use Example B after you get more experience reading your opponents.

SCENARIO 2

Now suppose all the players have $1,000 in chips, the blinds are $10 and $25, and you are on the button with:

Passive Paul, the first player after the big blind, limps in for $25. Aggressive Al raises to $200 and everyone passes to you on the button. The two blinds and Passive Paul can still act after you do before the flop.

How do you play your hand?

A. Move all in because aces are the best hand and the raiser will surely call.

B. Reraise to $400. The initial raiser will probably call your reraise and maybe even move in on you.

Analysis

Option B is our preferred play. Both of the blinds and Passive Paul will probably fold. Action Al, who raised to $200, is almost sure to call your raise. Heads-up against Al, your aces will have a better chance of holding up than they would in a multiway pot. Remember that we want some action with our pocket aces.

SCENARIO 3

Now suppose all the players have around $1,000 in chips except one poor soul who has only $250 left in his stack. The blinds are $10 and $25 and once again, you are on the button with:

The first two players after the big blind each limp in for $25. Novice Nancy, who is the short stack, moves in for her total $250.

How do you play your two Aces?
A. Move all in so you can isolate the short stack
B. Raise to $500
C. Smooth call the $250

Analysis
Option C would be the correct play in this scenario. There's no reason to blow the other players out by reraising since $250 is a very large raise when the blinds are only $10 and $25. It is much better to just call in the hope that you can pick up one of the other players ("picking up a player" means that someone else will enter the pot).

SCENARIO 4

Now suppose the blinds are $10 and $25 and all the players have about $1,000 in chips except poor pitiful you. You have only $275 left. Authority Artie limps in for $25 and Reckless Rick raises to $100. Sitting on the button with your measly $275, you see a ray of sunshine at the end of the tunnel—pocket aces at last!

How do you play your hand?

A. Smooth-call hoping to get other players to come in

B. Move all-in

Analysis

Both A and B could be correct. If you smooth-call, more players might come in, thus giving you a chance to win a big pot. The raiser will usually bet the flop, especially since you are short on chips. The raiser actually could help protect your hand against the other players in the pot if he bets after the flop.

Option B is correct because you're almost sure of getting called with a good chance of doubling up—and when you are short on chips, you're always looking for opportunities to double up. Option B is also safer than Option A because, with fewer players in the pot after you have raised them out of it, your chances of winning are greater.

How to Play Aces on the Flop

SCENARIO 5

Now suppose all the players have $1,000 in chips. Your hand is the A♥ A♠. You brought it in for $100, four times the size of the big blind, from first position. One player called the raise. The pot now contains the two blinds ($10 plus $25), your $100, and your opponent's $100 for a total of $235.

How do you play your pocket aces?

A. Bet $300 thinking he will surely call

B. Move in all your chips because you have a great hand

C. Check to give your opponent a chance to bet

Analysis

The preferred play is (C). This flop is so strong for your pocket aces that you want to give your lone opponent the opportunity to bluff. How do you do that? You check. If he also checks, you can always bet on fourth street, no matter what card comes off. Your only real danger with this flop is that your opponent might hit a lucky straight on the turn.

SCENARIO 6

All the players have $1,000 in chips. Your hand is:

You brought it in for $100, four times the size of the big blind, from first position. One player called the raise. The pot now contains the two blinds ($10 plus $25), your $100, and your opponent's $100 for a total of $235.

How do you play your pocket aces?

A. Move in all your chips because you have an overpair to all the cards on the flop.

B. Bet $300. You don't want to give your opponent a free card because of the possible straight and flush draws.

C. Check all the way because this is a dangerous flop.

Analysis

A bet is in order here (B). With two suited face cards on the flop, there are a variety of hands and draws that your opponent could call with. You don't want to give him a free card. Also, your opponent may call you with a king in his hand, which your pocket aces can beat.

SCENARIO 7

All the players have $1,000 in chips. Your hand is the A♥ A♠. You brought it in for $100, four times the size of the big blind, from first position. One player called the raise. The pot now contains the two blinds ($10 plus $25), your $100, and your opponent's $100 for a total of $235.

How do you play your pocket aces?

A. Bet all in because you are sure to have the best hand and don't want to give any free cards.

B. Check, hoping your opponent will bet. If he doesn't have the 4♥ in his hand, you have the best hand.

C. Check all the way to the river because he might have the 4♥ and you don't want to get busted.

Analysis

You should check (B). Unless your opponent is lucky enough to have the case four in his hand (the last four), you have the nuts. You want to give him a chance to make a pair, which would give him a lower full house than yours, or to make a bluff at the pot. It is very unlikely that he has a four in his hand since he called $100 to see the flop.

SCENARIO 8

All the players have $1,000 in chips. Your hand is:

You brought it in for $100, four times the size of the big blind, from first position. One player called the raise. The pot now contains the two blinds ($10 plus $25), your $100, and your opponent's $100 for a total of $235.

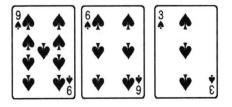

How do you play your pocket aces?

A. Check to give your opponent a chance to bet, because you have the top overpair and the nut flush draw.

B. Bet $300 because he might make a straight.

C. Bet all your chips because you have an overpair and surely the best hand.

Analysis

Option A is the preferred play. This is a very powerful flop for your aces, especially since you have the nut flush draw to go with your big overpair. Be prepared to go all in with this hand if necessary.

Playing Big Pairs: Kings

How to Play Kings Before the Flop

Pocket kings is the "other" real pair—only one hand is a favorite over two kings before the flop. We will usually play a pair of kings about the same way that we play pocket aces. We normally want to raise three to four times the big blind when we are the first player to enter the pot. We also want to get all of our chips in before the flop if possible.

If someone reraises your initial raise, it is almost always correct to reraise or move all-in, especially when you're still new to the game. You'll have the best starting hand except on the rare occasion when you run into aces. It's ugly, but there's nothing you can do about it when that happens—it's just part of the luck of the game.

Kings are very hard to fold before the flop—it takes an experienced player to be able to make this laydown. This is where practice at reading your opponents pays off. For instance, suppose a very solid player (whom you know never raises without a hand) raises three to four times the size of the big blind. Another player reraises him four times his initial raise. The solid player then moves in.

Sometimes, if you are concentrating and into the game,

you "know" without a doubt that the solid player has A-A.

When you get to the point that you are 90 percent sure that you are correct, you will be able to make the laydown.

In a famous hand at the World Series of Poker in 1992, Hamid Dastmalchi folded pocket kings when Mike Alsaadi reraised him before the flop. Dastmalchi showed the kings as he threw them in the muck and, in a gentlemanly gesture, Alsaadi showed the pocket aces he had raised with. Dastmalchi went on to win the World Championship of Poker for $1,000,000 and Alsaadi finished fourth for a win of $101,000.

SCENARIO 9

Now suppose you are in first position with:

The blinds are $10-$25. You bring it in for a normal raise of $75 and Tight Ted, sitting two seats to your left, calls. Everyone else folds to Reckless Rick on the button. Rick reraises to $200. Both of the blinds fold.

What's Your Move?
A. Reraise the pot to $600
B. Smooth call because you are afraid he has aces
C. Reraise all-in because your hand is so big

Analysis
With pocket kings, we want to get most of the money in before the flop. If we reraise to $600, Tight Ted will probably throw his hand away. Reckless Rick will probably call or maybe reraise. Smooth-calling is dangerous because Tight Ted may come in with something like A-K or a pair and hit the flop. Remember that your kings will hold up better against one player than two. If you move all in, Ted and Rick will likely throw their hands away unless they have the one hand that you don't want to see—pocket aces. We don't want to force them to throw away hands that we are a big favorite over.

Option (A) is the preferred play.

SCENARIO 10

Now suppose you are in the $25 big blind with:

The first three players limp in for $25 followed by the button and the small blind, making a total of five players already in the pot. The pot has $150 in it.

What's Your Move?

A. Check and see what comes on the flop

B. Move all your chips in and hope you can win it here

C. Raise the pot to $175

Analysis

You must raise to narrow the field (C). If you check, you're just asking for someone to outdraw your kings. Moving all-in will probably win the pot with no contest, but we want action with kings. Raising to $175 will probably narrow the field and give you a better chance of winning a decent pot.

SCENARIO 11

Now suppose Reckless Rick opens in first position for $125. Solid Sam, sitting in a middle position, calls. Everyone else folds to you on the button. You lost $600 a few hands earlier and only have $400 left in your stack. Your hand is:

What's Your Move?

A. Smooth-call and save your remaining $275 to bet on the flop if an ace doesn't come

B. Move all in with your chips

C. Raise to $250 to try and build a bigger pot

Analysis

You are now shortstacked with only $400 in chips. With Reckless Rick raising and Solid Sam calling, the pot has $285 in it. You are going to play this pot all the way and want to give yourself the best chance of winning it. The fewer players who get to see the flop, the better your chances are of winning. You move all in hoping to knock out as many players as you can. If everyone folds, you will pick up $285, a good improvement in your chip position, making Option (B) the preferred play.

How to Play Kings On the Flop

It seems like an overcard ace comes on the flop an inordinate number of times when you are holding a pair of kings. When an ace comes on the flop, someone holding something as weak as A-3 has a better hand than your kings. When an ace comes, you must play kings very cautiously.

SCENARIO 12

Now suppose you are in first position with:

You raised the pot before the flop to $100 and got called by Novice Nancy, who is sitting one spot behind you. Solid Sam also called on the button. Everyone else folded, making the pot $335. The flop comes:

You are first to act.

What's Your Move?
A. Bet the size of the pot $335
B. Check and then raise if someone bets
C. Check and see what the other players do

Analysis

We don't like the flop when an ace comes. It always slows us up when we have kings. Two aces on the flop looks better than one, because it is one less ace that the other players could have in their hand. We know that when Solid Sam comes into the pot, he has good cards, so he could easily have an ace in his hand. Knowing how she plays, we realize that Novice Nancy could also have an ace. We need more information.

Therefore, we choose Option (C). When you check on the flop, your opponents may think that you have an ace in your hand and you're slow-playing it. After all, you raised before the flop. By checking on the flop, you might freeze them from betting. If they also check on the flop, bet $200 on the turn—you might win the pot right there. If you get called, check on the river unless you catch a king, in which case you can bet.

SCENARIO 13

Now suppose you are in middle position with the K♠ K♦. You raised before the flop to $100 and got called by Loose Louie on the button and Tight Ted in the small blind. The pot has $325 in it. The flop comes:

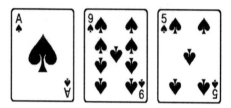

Tight Ted checks.

What's Your Move?

A. Check with the intention of moving in on Loose Louie if he bets

B. Bet about $300 to win the pot right now

C. Check with the intention of folding if someone bets

Analysis

Checking with the nut flush draw and an underpair (kings) against just two opponents, one of whom has already checked, is not the correct play. Loose Louie might bet behind us without having either an ace or a flush, putting us in a difficult situation trying to decide what to do. We bet $300 and try to win the pot on the flop (Option B). If Louie folds and Tight Ted moves in on us, we should probably fold unless Ted has only a few more chips than our bet. We will probably have to catch another spade to win against Ted. If we are called on the flop, we check fourth street unless a spade or a king comes.

Playing Big Pairs: Queens

How to Play Queens Before the Flop

Pocket queens is a hand that needs to be played with caution both before and after the flop. Many times, especially in the later rounds of a tournament, a classic confrontation comes up in which two players get all their chips in the pot before the flop. One player has A-K and the other player has Q-Q. The queens are the favorite, though only a small favorite, over the A-K. I have heard many a player drag his weary body out of the tournament area mumbling to himself over losing the hand with his pocket queens when an ace or king came at the river.

Queens also have two overpairs—aces and kings—that can be out against them before the flop. Then when an ace or king comes on the flop, you're always fearful that someone has hit his ace or king. Sometimes you will just have to take a chance and go with your pair of queens, either before or after the flop.

In early position we like to raise at least four times the big blind before the flop—we are trying to narrow the field. We want to weed out the players with overcards to give our pocket queens a better chance of holding up. You might even raise as much as five times the big blind if you are first to enter the pot.

SCENARIO 14

You are the first to act. Your hand is:

The blinds are $10-$25.

What's Your Move?
    A. Raise to $300
    B. Raise to $125
    C. Move all in

Analysis

If you move all in or make a large bet ($300 is a large bet when the blinds are this small), the only hands that will call you probably are aces or kings.

Therefore, Option (B) is the preferred play.

SCENARIO 15

Now suppose Solid Sam limped in first position and Reckless Rick limped behind him. You decide to make it $175 to go. They both call. You have:

They both check to you on the flop. It is:

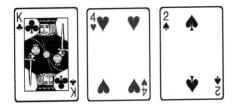

What's Your Play?

A. Check behind them and then bet on fourth street if it is checked again

B. Move all in to protect your hand

C. Bet around $350 to see if you have the best hand

Analysis

If you bet about $350, it would involve a huge amount of your stack, whereas checking the flop after raising pre-flop could appear to your opponents as though you are trying to trap them. Option A is your safest play. If everyone checks again on fourth street, bet about $250, an amount that you hope will deceive your opponents into thinking that you want them to call.

SCENARIO 16

Now suppose Solid Sam limped in first position and Reckless Rick limped behind him. You have the Q♠ Q♦ on the button. You raise four times the big blind, plus $25 for each of the limpers, making your total bet $150. Both blinds fold. Then Solid Sam reraises to $600 total. Reckless Rick folds.

What's Your Move?
  A. Move all in
  B. Call and look at the flop to see if a overcard comes
  C. Fold

Analysis

Whenever someone limps into the pot, you should make a mental note of it. Good players will often limp in early position with strong hands, hoping that someone will raise so that they can reraise. Since Solid Sam only comes in with premium cards and is willing to invest 60 percent of his stack, he must have your queens beaten. When he reraises, an A-K probably is the only hand that he could have that you could beat.

At this point, for you to call the raise would amount to the same thing as putting in all of your chips. Then you would have so much invested in the pot that you couldn't run away from it. On the other hand, if Sam had folded and Reckless Rick had reraised, you might have considered moving in on Rick. But against Sam, you should fold (C). You always need to adjust your play to the playing styles of your opponents.

How to Play Queens After the Flop

SCENARIO 17

Now suppose you are in late position next to the button with:

Before the flop, Action Al raises the pot to $100, Passive Paul calls behind Al, and everyone else folds to you. You reraise to $300. The blinds fold, but Al calls your raise and so does Paul. The pot now has $935 in it.

The flop comes:

Action Al is first to act and moves all in with the rest of his chips. Paul folds. Now it is up to you.

What's Your Move?
    A. Fold. Action Al probably has a straight
    B. Call

Analysis

In making your decision, you have to ask yourself some questions. What would Action Al move in with here? Maybe A-J, Q-J, or maybe with nothing. With his style of play he might just be trying to win the pot with a total bluff (absolutely nothing). If he had made a straight on the flop, he probably would just check and hope that someone bets behind him so that he can raise.

Next question: What is the strength of your hand? You have an overpair to the flop, plus an open-end straight draw.

After thinking it through, the answer becomes obvious. You must call (Option B).

SCENARIO 18

Now suppose you are in the big blind with the Q♠ Q♥. The players all fold around to Reckless Rick on the button. Rick raises to $100 and the small blind folds. You reraise him to $300 and he calls. The pot now has $610 in it. The flop comes:

It is your turn to act.

What's Your Move?
    A. Move in with your remaining $700
    B. Bet $300
    C. Check

Analysis
You are going to play this hand all the way. Reckless Rick is the type of player who might raise with any two cards and, if you show any kind of weakness in your play, he will bet. If you bet at him, he will probably fold. The flop is a safe one with no big draws—Rick would need to have a 4-3 in his hand to have an open-end straight draw. We give Rick more credit than just having a 4-3.

In order to make the maximum on this hand, check (C) and then raise all in if Rick bets. By checking you may deceive Rick into thinking that you have an A-K and missed the flop. In that case, he may try to steal the pot. Surprise him!

Playing Big Pairs: Jacks

How to Play Jacks Before the Flop

A pair of jacks is a hand that needs to be played with extreme caution both before and after the flop. Jacks can run into a pair of aces, kings or queens before the flop and when an ace, king or queen comes on the flop, you will fear that someone has hit an overcard.

In the early rounds of a tournament, try not to play a big pot with pocket jacks unless you flop a set (three of a kind).

SCENARIO 19

Suppose Solid Sam opens in first position for $100. Novice Nancy calls $100 and Authority Artie also calls $100. You are sitting on the button with:

You also call the $100. The small blind folds. Tight Ted, the big blind, announces "I'm all in!" and moves his chips to the middle. Authority Artie starts complaining: "Oh no," he yaps, "the tight player has moved in—he must have aces. What a waste it would be to put any more money in the pot." Ignoring him, Solid Sam calls all-in. Novice Nancy folds. And, still complaining, Authority Artie folds.

It is back to you. The pot now has $2,310 in it.

What's Your Move?
A. Call with your remaining $900
B. Fold

Analysis
With this much betting and the type of players putting in the bets, your jacks should be beaten before the flop. You could get lucky, of course, and hit a set on the flop, but do you really want to put your chips in when you have to hit a jack to stay alive? It would be much better to save the $900 for another hand.

As for Authority Artie, he should learn to be quiet while the hand is going on. It is very poor etiquette at the poker table for players to voice opinions about the play of others. While action is going on, players should watch but aren't suppose to guess everyone's hole cards out loud, because it could influence the play.

Your best move is Option (B).

SCENARIO 20

Now suppose you are in the large blind with:

Solid Sam raises the pot to $100 in first position and everyone folds around to Reckless Rick on the button. He calls, the small blind folds, and now it's your turn to act.

What's Your Move?
A. Raise to $300
B. Move all-in
C. Just call

Analysis
Two jacks is a good hand but one that must be played with caution. Since Solid Sam raised from up front, it is quite possible that he has a larger pair than jacks. Reckless Rick is capable of playing lots of hands and, since he didn't reraise, we will assume that he doesn't have a pair higher than jacks. We want to look at the flop and then make the best decision as to how to play our pocket jacks.

Therefore, just calling (C) is the best move.

SCENARIO 21

You have:

The flop comes:

Since you are in the big blind, you are the first to act after the flop with your pocket jacks. Solid Sam is next, followed by Reckless Rick on the button. The pot has $310 in it.

What's Your Move?
A. Bet $300
B. Move all-in
C. Check

First Move Analysis

We have an overpair to the flop, which is good, but we don't have any idea where Solid Sam is. We know that he probably has a strong hand because he raised before the flop from first position. So, we check the flop (C) and see what Sam does. After we check, Sam checks. Then

Reckless Rick bets $300.

What's the best move?
A. Fold
B. Call
C. Raise all-in

Second Move Analysis
When Solid Sam checked the flop, he told us that he probably has two overcards, maybe A-K. Reckless Rick could have anything, but we don't mind playing against him. There is a good chance that our jacks is a better hand than Rick's hand. If we just call the $300, we are committed to the pot anyway. Therefore it is better to move in (C) and try to blow Solid Sam and Rick out of the pot to try to win a nice pot right here.

Playing Middle Pairs

How to Play 10-10 through 7-7

The lower the pair the more dangerous it becomes to play. The main danger, of course, is that an opponent is holding a higher pair. You don't want to put a lot of chips in before the flop with these middle pairs because, even if you flop a set, there is the possibility than an opponent has flopped a larger set if the board comes with overcards.

When you flop three of a kind you have a strong hand, one that you are usually going to play all the way even if you get beaten. When you hit a set, just play your hand in a way that will get as many chips in the pot as possible.

As a beginning player, play pairs of tens through sevens strongly only when you flop a set. Remember that any card that comes that is higher than your pair could make a higher set for someone. Sometimes the flop comes with cards that give you a straight draw. For example, you could have 7-7 and the flop comes 4-5-6, giving you an open-end straight draw with an overpair. Or suppose you have two tens in your hand and the flop comes Q-J-9. You have an open-end straight draw, but it is a dangerous draw because of the two overcards on the board.

SCENARIO 22

You are in the big blind with:

Novice Nancy raises the pot to $75 in first position and Tight Ted calls one spot in front of the button. Reckless Rick calls on the button. The small blind folds. Now it is your turn.

What's Your Move?
A. Raise to $200
B. Fold
C. Call

Before the Flop Analysis
You have a pair of nines, but there are lots of pairs and overcards to nines. You don't want to raise because one of the other players might have a larger pair. Since you are last to act, no one can reraise you before the flop if you just call. Calling to see the flop (C) is your best play.

Now suppose the flop comes:

With $310 in the pot...

What's Your Move?
    A. Bet $300
    B. Move all-in
    C. Check

After the Flop Analysis - First Move

You have flopped trip nines. Only one hand can beat you at this time, three aces. There is no flush draw on the flop, but there is a gutshot (inside) straight draw. For example, if someone has a 5-3 in his hand, he needs a deuce to make a straight. But this is a remote possibility since the pot was raised before the flop.

Since there aren't any good draws out against you, you are going to slow-play (C) your set of nines in the hope that the other players put lots of chips in the pot after you check so that you can check-raise.

After you check the flop, Novice Nancy also checks, Tight Ted bets $300, and Reckless Rick folds. It is up to you.

What's Your Move?
    A. Raise all-in
    B. Call
    C. Raise to $600
    D. Fold

After the Flop Analysis - Second Move

You are very happy with your hand and want to get the maximum money in this pot. Tight Ted probably has an ace with a big kicker. If he does, he is drawing very weak against your trips. You are going to smooth-call (B). You're hoping that Novice Nancy also calls behind you. Your play is to wait until fourth street (the turn) to try to trap Ted for the rest of his chips (and perhaps trap Nancy, too).

Chris Moneymaker, the 2003 World Champion of Poker, won his seat in the Big One via a $39 online satellite. Prior to his win, he had played no-limit Texas hold'em in online tournaments only.

SCENARIO 23

Now suppose Tight Ted limps in first position. You are sitting to his left with:

What's Your Move?
    A. Fold
    B. Raise to $125
    C. Limp

First Move Analysis

Your pocket tens is not a strong pair, especially after Tight Ted limps in suspiciously. You want to look at the flop as cheaply as possible in the hope of flopping a set. Limping (C) is the correct play.

After you call, Authority Artie limps behind you. Then Action Al raises the pot to $150. Everyone folds around to Tight Ted, who reraises to $400.

What's Your Move?
    A. Call
    B. Fold
    C. Move all in

Second Move Analysis

With Tight Ted limping into the pot from up front and then reraising Action Al, you have to give him credit for a better hand than yours. Fold to fight another day (B).

Playing Small Pairs

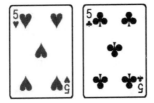

Playing 6-6 through 2-2

When you have a small pair, you have even more overcards to worry about. With these small pairs, you will be looking at the flop only if you can get in cheap. After you see the flop, you will only play a large pot if you flop a set. Otherwise, you don't want to put any more money in the pot.

SCENARIO 24

Suppose you are in the big blind with:

Novice Nancy opens in second position for $50, Loose Louie calls to her left, Action Al calls on the button, and Authority Artie calls from the small blind.

What's Your Move?
A. Fold
B. Raise to $150
C. Call

First Move Analysis
You have a pair of fives, not the kind of pair that you want to put a lot of chips in the pot with before the flop, although you can call a small amount to try to hit trips on the flop. The correct play is to call (C). "Please give me a five on the flop!" you're silently praying.

The flop comes with the:

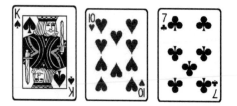

Authority Artie checks, we check, and Nancy bets $100. Louie folds. Al calls on the button and Artie folds in the small blind.

What's Your Move?
    A. Call
    B. Raise
    C. Fold

Second Move Analysis
Ooops! You didn't hit the set you were hoping for. No set on the flop, no bet. The correct strategy is to fold (C).

Big Connected Cards

How to Play A-K

Otherwise known as Big Slick, A-K is a hand that plays a lot of big pots. You usually raise with A-K, thereby putting pressure on your opponents. It isn't unusual to see a player raise before the flop with a pair only to have an opponent reraise all-in behind him with an A-K.

You might ask, "Why would someone move all in with this hand?" Big Slick is primarily a drawing hand and any pair is a favorite to it before the flop. It is because of the pressure that you put on players when you move in on them with A-K. For example, suppose an opponent raises the pot with J-J and you move all-in with enough chips to cover his stack. Your opponent feels a ton of pressure because if he loses the hand he will be out of the tournament. He is at a disadvantage because he doesn't know what cards you are holding. Unless he has aces, he knows that if you have a larger pair than his jacks, you are a big favorite to win the pot.

And that is the kind of pressure inherent to no-limit hold'em tournaments—if you make the wrong decision, you instantly become a spectator looking on from the rail.

Lots of tournaments are won or lost in confrontations between an A-K and a pair. As T.J. Cloutier wrote in *Championship No-Limit & Pot-Limit Hold'em*, "You have to win when you have A-K and you win when you're up against A-K." When your A-K is up against a pocket pair, it is almost like flipping coins—heads you win, tails you lose. A classic confrontation that seems to inevitably occur in tournaments is A-K against Q-Q, in which the queens are a small favorite against Big Slick. In fact, unless an opponent has pocket aces or kings, the A-K is only a small underdog in the pot. For that simple reason, A-K is a hand that players try to bully the table with.

The higher the blinds get in the tournament the more you can put pressure on your opponents when you have an A-K. In the early rounds there isn't much money to fight over, but in the later rounds just winning the blinds and antes will help you to maintain your stack size.

In the late stages of a tournament, a lot of players will play any type of ace-hand, regardless of the second card in their hand. On television you often will see two opponents hit an ace on the flop. What determines the winner is the kicker, the side card you have in your hand. If you have A-K, you have the highest possible kicker, aces with a king kicker, which would beat an opponent with A-J or A-Q unless he paired his kicker. And that is another strength of Big Slick.

Of course, if your A-K is suited you can make a flush (the nut flush, in fact) or you can make the nut straight if the board is showing a Q-J-10. One of the beauties of A-K suited, then, is that when you flop a flush or straight draw, you are always drawing to the best hand.

SCENARIO 25

Suppose you are on the button with:

The blinds are $10-$25. Solid Sam opens for $100 and Tight Ted calls to his left. Everyone folds to you on the button.

What's Your Move?
A. Call
B. Fold
C. Raise to $300

Analysis
Big Slick is a playable hand in a lot of situations, but this time two of your opponents have already entered the pot for a raise. Further, you know from observing their playing styles that neither of them ordinarily enters a pot without a premium hand. If one of them has A-A or K-K, you would be a huge dog.

Your best strategy is to fold (B). You have nothing invested, why get involved?

SCENARIO 26

Now suppose you are on the button with:

With the blinds at $10-$25, Action Al brings it in for a raise of $100 from first position. Loose Louie calls behind him and everyone else folds to you.

What's Your Move?
A. Call
B. Fold
C. Raise to $300

Analysis
Your A-K looks better in this scenario because neither Action Al nor Loose Louie necessarily have to have big hands to enter the pot. Naturally, either of them could have a big hand, but you know that they are very capable of playing cards that are inferior to your A-K. You've seen them play hands like A-J, A-Q, and K-Q in similar situations. If the flop comes with an ace, they will be in trouble if they are holding an ace with a lower kicker. Ditto for a flop with a king in it.

Your best strategy is to call and see the flop (A).

Big Connected Cards

How to Play A-Q

In the early stages of the tournament while the blinds are low, limp with A-Q when you are in early position. A-Q is a hand you can get in trouble with when an ace comes on the flop and someone else has A-K, giving them a better kicker. When you are next to or on the button and no one has entered the pot, raise to three or four times the size of the big blind.

The value of A-Q changes as the blinds increase. You will hold only so many premium hands during a tournament and, in order to stay alive in the higher rounds, you will have to pick up some blinds and antes. Although A-Q isn't a premium hand, it is one that you can raise with after the blinds get higher. You can start making a normal raise of three to four times the big blind after the blinds reach the $50-$100 and higher levels.

Before you raise with A-Q, take into account your opponents' style of play. For example, do they defend their blinds or will they give them up without a fight? This is a very important factor to consider. (If you have an ace or queen in your hand, it lowers the chance that other players have a pair of aces or queens.) This is the type of hand that you can play strongly when you are in trouble and need to make a move.

SCENARIO 27

Suppose you are in first position with:

Tthe blinds are $10-$25, and you have $1,000 in chips.

What's Your Move?
    A. Raise to $100
    B. Fold
    C. Limp

Analysis

At these low levels you want to limp (C) with an A-Q because there isn't enough money in the pot to risk someone reraising you. Too many players are yet to act after you if you raise, and someone might wake up with a hand.

If you limp, your opponents might be afraid you have limped with A-A and therefore decide not to raise you. If you hit a good flop, you're in clover for a cheap price.

SCENARIO 28

Suppose you are in first position with:

The blinds are $200-$400 with $25 ante. The pot has $825 in blind and ante money. You have $4,000 in chips.

What's Your Move?
A. Limp
B. Fold
C. Raise to $1,200
D. Move all-in

Analysis
The pot now has some money to fight over. The blinds and antes ($825) amount to about 20 percent of your $4,000 stack. In Scenario 1, with only $35 blind money in the middle, the pot amounted to only about 3.5 percent of your $1,000 stack. Now you can see how your chip position improves just by winning the blinds and antes when they get higher.

Use option (C) to try to pick up the pot.

SCENARIO 29

Now suppose you are in first position:

The blinds are $300-$600 with a $50 ante. The pot now has $1,400 from the blinds and antes. You have $3,000 in chips. It's $600 to you.

What's Your Move?
    A. Limp
    B. Fold
    C. Raise to $1,800
    D. Move all-in

Analysis

In this situation it is costing you $1,400 for every round you play. In two rounds you will be almost broke. You need to improve your chip status. If you make a normal raise of between $1,800 and $2,400, you will be committed to the pot anyway.

Since you aren't going to fold, move all in (D) to try to win the pot now, and to keep your opponents from thinking they can make you fold any time they reraise you.

Big Connected Cards

How to Play A-J

Ace-jack is another trouble hand, one that you will be playing sometimes, but very cautiously. You usually cannot call big bets with A-J. If someone raises the pot in front of you, you usually are wise to just fold unless you are in serious chip trouble. An A-J is even more dangerous than an A-Q because the jack is a lower kicker than the queen.

From front to middle position, you can limp with A-J. From late position, you can make the normal raise of 3-4 times the big blind if no one has come into the pot. Keep in mind how aggressive the players in the blind are. If they are very aggressive players, just limp to try to keep from involving too many of your chips in case one of them raises.

Even for very experienced players, A-J is a very tough hand to play. With A-J you are looking for flops like K-Q-10, 5-J-J, and A-A-J.

SCENARIO 30

Suppose you are in the $25 big blind with:

Tight Ted raises the pot to $100 in early position and everyone folds to you in the big blind.

What's Your Move?
A. Call
B. Reraise to $300
C. Fold

Analysis
You don't want to put much money into the pot with an A-J, especially against a tight player like Ted. You don't want to flop a pair of aces and get into trouble against Ted's better kicker.

Folding (C) is the correct play.

SCENARIO 31

Now suppose the blinds are $200-$400 with a $25 ante. The pot has $850 in it before anyone acts on his hand. You are on the button with:

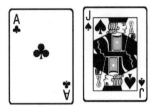

You have $2400 in chips. Everyone folds except Reckless Rick, sitting immediately to your right, who limps for $400.

What's Your Move?
A. Limp
B. Fold
C. Raise to $1,200
D. Move all-in

Analysis
Except in a few situations, an A-J isn't a hand that you want to invest a lot of money with. This is one of those few situations— you are short on chips and need to improve your position. Since Rick didn't raise in front of you, his hand is probably weaker than yours. With a normal raise of $1,200-$1,600, you are committed to the pot anyway.

So, just move all in (D) and hope to win the pot right there.

Big Connected Cards

How to Play K-Q

If A-J is difficult for even experienced players to play, K-Q is even trickier because there are more chances for you to get into kicker trouble with it. If you hit a queen on the flop, you have two queens with a king kicker while an opponent could have queens with an ace kicker. What you are looking for is the flop to come J-10-9, A-J-10, or K-K-Q. With these flops, you would have the nuts—and the nuts is exactly what we want to show down at the end of the hand.

In the early rounds of the tournament, you can limp from up front and from middle position with K-Q when you are playing at a table where your opponents aren't doing a lot of pre-flop raising. You can make the normal raise of three to four times the big blind when you are on the button or one seat to the button's immediate right— but only if the blinds are tight players who might fold and give up their blinds.

SCENARIO 32

Now suppose you are in the $25 big blind with:

Passive Paul raises the pot to $50, Action Al calls in middle position, and Tight Ted calls on the button. The small blind folds and now it's your turn to act.

What's Your Move?
A. Fold
B. Raise to $150
C. Call

Analysis

K-Q isn't a hand you want to be calling large raises with. Tight Ted called the small raise but he didn't reraise. He probably wouldn't reraise unless he had a large pair. Most likely, Ted has some kind of pocket pair and is hoping to flop a set, or he may have an A-J, A-Q, or even A-K. Action Al might call with lots of different hands in the hope of catching a good flop. Passive Paul doesn't do much raising, but doubling the big blind isn't much of a raise.

Just call (C) and look at the flop. It doesn't cost you much to try to catch a good one.

SCENARIO 33

Now suppose you are on the button with $3,500 in chips. The blinds are $200-$400 with a $25 ante. The pot has $850 in it, Everyone folds to you on the button. In the $400 big blind is Tight Ted with $3,500 in chips, and in the $200 small blind with $4,000 in chips is Passive Paul.

You have:

What's Your Move?
A. Move all-in
B. Call the $400
C. Raise to $1,200

Analysis
Although K-Q isn't a big hand, you are in a little bit of chip trouble. The best thing here is that you have two players in the blinds who will not call a raise unless they have a good hand. You like having tight and passive players in the blinds.

The correct play is to raise to $1,200 (C). If either Ted or Paul picks up a premium hand, he probably will reraise. If that happens, fold because you know he most likely has a better hand than K-Q.

SCENARIO 34

Now suppose the blinds are $300-$600 with a $50 ante. The pot has $1,400 in it. You have $2,400 in chips and you are the first to act.

This is you hand:

What's Your Move?
    A. Fold
    B. Call
    C. Raise to $1,800
    D. Move all-in

Analysis
You are in big chip trouble—you're in the Move-In Zone on the Betting Chart. You can't take the blinds and antes twice without going broke. If you go through the blinds, you will be so shortstacked that players will start calling you with marginal hands.

Even though K-Q usually isn't that strong a hand, the correct play is to move all in (D) in order to give yourself a chance to survive.

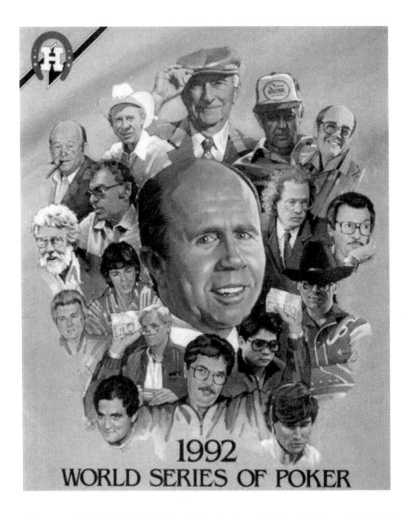

The cover of the 1992 World Series of Poker brochure featuring drawings of the World Champions of Poker from 1970-1991. Clockwise from the top are Johnny Moss, Sailor Roberts, Doyle Brunson, Bobby Baldwin, Bill Smith, Tom McEvoy, Johnny Chan, Phil Hellmuth, Brad Daugherty, Hamid Dastmalchi, Berry Johnston, Jack Keller, Stu Ungar, Jack Straus, Hal Fowler, Puggy Pearson, and Amarillo Slim Preston. In the center is Jack Binion. Daugherty was featured in the brochure as the reigning champion.

PART NINE

Tournament Practice Flops

How to Read, Bet & Play On the Flop

Being able to read the flop correctly is critical in determining the strength of your hand and how to play it. In no-limit hold'em, it is especially important to play correctly on the flop because so few hands are played to the river. Most experienced no-limit players prefer winning the pot in one of two places—either before the flop or on the flop.

When you hear a player say, "I couldn't tell where I was at in the hand," he means that he had trouble deciding how strong his hand was in relation to the cards on the flop and the cards that his opponent(s) might be holding. "I had trouble putting Joe on a hand," means that, based on his opponent's actions before the flop and on the flop, it was difficult to determine the strength of Joe's hole cards.

In this section we will show you some flops and lead you through a thought process that will help you to determine how to bet and play certain types of hands when various types of flop are dealt.

Keep in mind that the following factors always affect how you play and bet any hand you are dealt:

- The betting action before the flop
- The strength of your hand
- The betting action in front of you on the flop
- The number of players who can act after you
- The nature of your opponents

Now let's look at some practice flops and go through a thought process that will lead to the best possible decision on how to play and bet several types of hands for each flop.

As you look at each flop, ask yourself:

- What is the nut hand for this flop?
- What are the possible drawing hands that would make the nuts on the turn or river?
- Who might have the best hand or a draw to it?

We use the player types listed in Part Three as short-cuts to describe the opponents you will be facing on each of the following tournament flops. In each of the following scenarios, you have $1,000 in chips. The blinds are $10-$25 and you are playing in the first round of the tournament.

Flop One

One High Card/Two Low Cards/Unsuited

SCENARIO 35

You are sitting in middle position with:

You raised to $100 before the flop. Only the Big Blind called, making a $210 pot. You have flopped *top pair/top kicker*. On the flop, the Big Blind checks to you.

What's Your Move?

Analysis

Two kings with an ace kicker is a fairly strong hand. Since you are against only one player, there's a good chance that you have the best hand at this time unless your opponent flopped a set. It is unlikely that he flopped two pair unless he's a loose player who might call a raise with an 8-7, K-8 or K-7 suited.

The Strategy We Suggest

If he checks to you, bet $150-$250. If he makes a normal bet ($150-$250 for this $210 pot), move in on him. If he makes a small bet ($50, for example), raise him four to six times the amount that he bet ($200-$300).

SCENARIO 36

The flop:

You are sitting in first position after the blinds with:

You raised to $100 before the flop and got called by the player to your left, the button, and the big blind for a total pot of $410. You have flopped *top trips*.

How would you bet and play them to maximize your profits?

Analysis
Your main concern is how to get the most chips into this pot. You have very few possible drawing hands to worry about.

The Strategy We Suggest
You have flopped *top trips,* a very strong hand on this K-8-7 flop. The only possible draws are a straight draw and a backdoor flush draw. Everyone in the pot has $900

in chips at this point. You would love to be able to get all your chips in at this time, but if you bet anything close to the size of the pot, there is a good chance that everyone will throw their hands away.

If you strongly believe that someone sitting behind you will bet, you can slow-play by checking. If you're not fairly sure that someone will bet if you check, make a small bet of $100-$200. Either way you hope that your opponents will sense weakness on your part and will put in lots of chips trying to steal the pot. It is a very nice feeling to have someone make a large bet at the pot when you are sitting there with the nuts.

SCENARIO 37

The flop:

You are in the big blind in an unraised pot holding:

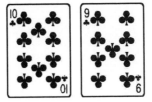

Two other players are in the pot with you—the small blind and the player next to the button—for a total pot of $75. The small blind checks to you on the K-8-7 flop.

How would you play your straight draw in this scenario?

Analysis

If you decide to make a small bet and get raised a substantial amount, you must fold your drawing hand. If you check and the player next to the button makes a small bet, you can call.

The Strategy We Suggest

At this point we don't have a made hand, only an open-ended straight draw. We have two choices in how to play this hand: Check hoping to get a free card and make our straight, or make a bet at the pot. We prefer to bet $50-$75 because we might win here with no calls. If someone calls we might hit our straight and win a big pot when we have the nuts.

Remember that you don't want to put a lot of chips in at this point on the flop because you only have a draw.

SCENARIO 38

The flop:

You are sitting to the right of the button holding:

The opening player, Action Al, raised the pot to $75 before the flop. You flat-called the raise and so did Authority Artie in the big blind. The pot now has $235 in it.

How do you play your bottom trips on the K-8-7 flop?

Analysis

You have flopped *bottom trips,* a very strong hand and the nuts at this point—unless someone has flopped a larger set. The only obvious draw is the straight draw, or possibly, a backdoor flush draw. Someone also could have a higher pair than your sevens and hit it to make a larger set. We are definitely going to play this hand all the way.

The Strategy We Suggest

If Artie (the big blind) checks and Al (the original raiser) bets, we are going to just smooth-call hoping to also pick up Artie in the big blind. If Artie bets out $150, for example, and Action Al calls, then we would raise to $400. If they both check to us, then we would bet about $200.

SCENARIO 39

The flop:

You are on the button holding:

Before the flop, Tight Ted raised to $100 from an early position. Solid Sam just called the raise from middle position. You also just called on the button.

On the flop, Tight Ted checks and Solid Sam bets $150.

What's your move with your underpair?

Analysis

Two jacks is a very dangerous hand in no-limit hold'em. If an overcard to your jacks comes on the flop and someone bets, it is almost always correct to fold your hand.

The Strategy We Suggest

Fold your hand. With Tight Ted raising before the flop and Solid Sam calling his raise, you know they both have a good hand. One of them is a big favorite to have a better hand than your two jacks so just give it up. Tight Ted might have even slow-played a set or checked A-K, wanting some action.

When these two players came in before the flop, you were looking to make a set of jacks, hoping they each had an ace-high hand so that you could win a big pot against them. If the flop had come with three undercards to your jacks, then you could have bet about the size of the pot in the hope that they both had an A-K or A-Q, for example, and you could win it on the flop.

Flop Two

Two High Cards/One Low Card/Suited

In each of the following scenarios, you have $1,000 in chips. The blinds are $10-$25 and you're playing in the first round of the tournament.

The flop comes:

SCENARIO 40

The flop comes:

You are sitting in late position just to the right of the button holding:

Before the flop, two players limped into the pot, you also limped, and the big blind checked, making a total pot of $110. On the flop, the big blind checks, the first limper checks, and the next player bets $100. You have flopped second pair with the nut flush draw.

What's Your Move?

Analysis

You don't want to risk going broke with this hand by making a big bet or raise on the flop. You have the second highest board pair, plus the nut flush draw. In other words, you have a lot of ways to improve your hand on the turn or river.

Try to play this hand cheap until you do improve.

The Strategy We Suggest

You have flopped the nut flush draw and middle pair, you probably don't have the best hand at this point. We suggest that you just call the $100 because you do have a good draw. If you make your nut flush or hit another queen, you might win a big pot.

The championship table at the 1991 World Series of Poker. From the dealer's left: Don Williams, fourth place; Robert Veltri, third place; Brad Daugherty, bracelet winner; and Don Holt, runner-up.

SCENARIO 41

The flop:

You are in late position holding:

Before the flop, you raised to $75. Loose Larry called on the button, and the big blind also called your raise. The pot now has $235 in it. You have flopped top two pair. Now the big blind checks to you.

What's Your Move?

Analysis

You now have top two pair, but on this flop there also is a possible flush draw and a gutshot straight draw. Loose Larry likes to gamble a lot. If Larry or the big blind has caught any part of the flop, he will probably call if you bet. Larry might even raise. If you go to the turn with this hand, it is possible that the fourth-street card will give one of your opponents a flush, or a flush draw if he has only one spade in his hand.

One of them could even have a gutshot straight draw on the flop.

The Strategy We Suggest

Bet about $200. Winning right on the flop would be just fine with you.

Brad Daugherty and Don Holt shaking hands at the conclusion of the 1991 WSOP championship event. In the background with his arms raised is Daugherty's "cheerleader," Hans "Tuna" Lund.

SCENARIO 42

The flop:

You are sitting two seats to the left of the big blind with:

Before the flop, you are the first player to come in—you raised to $100. You got called by Reckless Rick, who had already lost a previous pot. Rick had only $400 left after calling your $100 raise. With just the two of you in the $235 pot, you flop *top pair/top kicker.*

What's Your Move?

Analysis

You are first to act and Reckless Rick must act after you. You know that you're going to play this hand out, so you ask yourself these questions: How can I get the most money in on the flop? What would Rick do if I checked? What would he do if I bet into him?

The Strategy We Suggest

Check to Rick—he will probably just move in because of his fast playing style.

SCENARIO 43

The flop:

Solid Sam is sitting to the left of the big blind and limps in for $25. We are next to act and look down at:

You raise to $125 with your pocket rockets, Action Al calls on the button, and the limper Solid Sam also calls the raise. With three of you in the $410 pot, the flop comes with an ace. You have flopped trip aces! Solid Sam checks to you.

What's Your Move?

Analysis

You have *top trips*—a very strong hand—but not as strong as it would be if the flush draw and gutshot straight draw were not on board. Anyone with even one spade in his hand could make a backdoor flush and beat you.

The Strategy We Suggest

You don't want someone who has only one spade in his hand to backdoor a flush. You cannot allow them to draw for free, so you are going to bet at least $300. You want to make them pay something to try to draw out on your hand. If you get raised, you will have to put the rest of your chips in the pot.

Flop Three

Three Middle Cards/Unsuited

The flop comes:

SCENARIO 44

You are sitting in the big blind with:

Suppose you started this hand with $1,000. The blinds are $10-$25. The button and the small blind limped in. After the flop the small blind checks to you.

What's Your Move?

Analysis

You now have top pair with a big kicker. It's not a superstrong hand, but there's a good chance that it is the best hand on the flop.

If someone has 10-8, 6-8, or 5-6, they would have an open-end straight draw. There also is the possibility that someone has a gutshot straight draw or a backdoor flush draw. Also, someone could hit a card that would make an overpair to your nines.

The Strategy We Suggest

After the small blind checks, we will bet $75, which is the size of the pot. We prefer to just win it at this point. If someone calls, you need to play cautiously—you don't want to play a large pot with this hand.

SCENARIO 45

The flop:

You have been dealt this hand in the big blind:

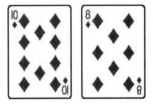

Suppose you started this hand with $1,000 in chips. The blinds are $10-$25. Before the flop, Tight Ted limped in middle position, Loose Larry limped on the button and the small blind limped.

The pot now has $100 in it.

What's Your Move?

Analysis

You now have a open-end straight draw. We can play the hand in one of two ways. First, we could lead into the pot for $100 and hope to pick it up there. If we get called we have a chance of making our hand and possibly winning a good pot. Or we could check in the hope of getting a free card to make our straight.

Knowing the playing style of your opponents and

having a good idea of the actions they might make will be an influence on how you play the hand.

The Strategy We Suggest

Lead into the pot for $100 and possibly pick it up right here. However, you must fold if someone makes a large raise.

T.J. Cloutier (r) and Tom McEvoy, co-authors of *Championship No-Limit & Pot-Limit Hold'em*, at Foxwoods Casino, where they placed first and second in the pot-limit hold'em tournament.

SCENARIO 46

The flop is:

You are sitting in early position holding:

Suppose you started this hand with $1,000. The blinds are $10-$25. You raise to $100, Tight Ted calls on the button and Loose Larry calls from the big blind. The pot now has $310 in it. Larry leads out and bets $200 on the 9-7-4 flop.

You are next to act.

What's Your Move?

Analysis

You now have an overpair of jacks, a good hand with this flop. You have to ask yourself what Tight Ted might have when he called your raise before the flop. There is a good chance that he has A-K or A-Q suited, or possibly a pair of tens or some other pair.

If he had an overpair to our jacks, Ted probably would

have reraised before the flop. Loose Larry would bet a variety of hands, including a drawing hand.

The Strategy We Suggest

Raise to $500 because you believe that your jacks is the best hand at the moment. Also, you don't want Tight Ted to take a card off (call) with a hand such as A-K and catch an ace or a king on the turn card.

Flop Four

Three High Cards/Unsuited

The flop:

SCENARIO 47

The flop:

You are sitting next to the button. Before the flop, Tight Ted opens the pot for $100. We look down to find:

Everybody folds to you. You decide to reraise to $300. The button and blinds fold. Tight Ted thinks about it and then calls.

On the flop, Ted checks.

What's Your Move?

Analysis

You realize that Ted doesn't play anything except premium cards, especially from early position. The nut hand on this flop is an A-Q, the only hand that can beat you at this point.

Chances are good that Ted doesn't have A-A because he didn't reraise before the flop. It is more likely that he has A-K or possibly a pair of queens, jacks or tens. This means that you are probably going to get good action with this hand.

The Strategy We Suggest

Including the blinds, there is $635 in the pot. you and Ted each have $700 left. When Ted checks on the flop, move $300 into the middle. If he has A-Q, A-K or trips, he will probably push in the rest of his chips. If Ted has Q-Q, he probably will either fold or move all in. If he has any other hand, it is likely that he will fold.

SCENARIO 48

The flop:

You are sitting in the small blind holding:

Before the flop, Solid Sam limped in from first position for $25 and Loose Louie also limped on the button. You completed the small blind to $25 and the Big Blind checked, bringing the pot to a total of $100. After the K-J-10 flop is dealt, you are first to act in the small blind.

What's Your Move?

Analysis

With four of you in the pot, you have flopped top pair with a good kicker and an open-end straight draw. Naturally you're afraid of an A-Q or a Q-9 because you know that if an opponent has one of those hands, he has flopped a straight and you're beaten. But since this is an unraised pot, it seems unlikely that someone has an A-Q.

It is more likely that a Q-9 will be out. Your hand looks pretty strong. The only person you might be afraid of is the limper, who may have limped in with a big hand trying to set a trap. Remember, too, that Loose Louie likes to bet.

The Strategy We Suggest

You are a little bit afraid of Solid Sam, who limped in first position. Check to see what Sam does. If he bets, you have to be very cautious because he probably has you beaten at this point, and you might need to hit the straight to win. Therefore we suggest that you fold if he makes a large bet.

If Sam checks, you can be pretty sure that Loose Louie will bet. Now it's your turn to have some fun—check-raise about three times the size of Louie's bet. If he bet $100, you bet $300. If he brought it in for $50, raise four times the bet to $200. If neither Sam nor Larry bets on the flop, lead on the turn so long as the turn card isn't a scary card such as a queen.

SCENARIO 49

The flop:

You are sitting two seats in front of the blinds with:

As the first player to enter the pot, you bring it in for $100. Reckless Rick reraises $100. It's $200 to call. Both blinds fold. You just call for the extra $100, bringing the pot to $435.

You're first to act.

What's Your Move?

Analysis

You have flopped top pair with top kicker and you also have a gutshot straight draw. Reckless Rick loves to raise, and there are a lot of hands with which he could raise on this flop. One of them is A-Q, a hand that he is quite capable of reraising with before the flop. But if he's been paying attention to his opponents, Rick remembers that you have been playing only premium cards and he should give you credit for a big hand.

The Strategy We Suggest

Check to Rick and see what he does. If he bets $200-$300, move in on him. Why fool around? If you just call, you're pot-logged anyway. By going all-in, you shut down the action. You have no more decisions to make. You're leaving the last decision up to Rick. If he has a big hand, he'll call. If he doesn't have a hand, you'll win a nice pot. As you get more mileage under your belt, you may want to explore other options on this type of hand, but for now let's keep it simple.

SCENARIO 50

The flop:

You are sitting in the big blind with:

Loose Larry opens in second position for $75 and Passive Paul calls on the button. The little blind calls. You just call the extra $50 from the big blind. The pot has $300 in it. The flop comes K-J-10. The small blind checks.

What's Your Move?

Analysis

We have flopped the nuts! Now our biggest decision is, "How can I get the most money into the pot?" We're almost sure that Loose Larry will bet if we check. We know that everybody likes to gamble with Larry, so they sometimes will call his bets with weaker hands than they would call anybody else with.

The Strategy We Suggest

This is a good spot to slow-play. We can accomplish this by checking. We check because we're pretty sure that Larry will bet and the other two players will call. If Larry bets $300 or less, and if one or more of the other players comes in, we will raise an amount that is double his bet (making it $600 if he bets $300, for example). If he makes a large bet of $500-$600 and no one calls, we will smooth-call on the flop. Then we will check the turn in the hope that he moves in. If he does not bet on the turn, we will bet into him on the river.

Flop Five

A Low Pair with a Suited Card

The flop:

SCENARIO 51

The flop:

You are sitting one seat in front of the button with:

Action Al raises to $75 from second position. Three players fold to you sitting one seat in front of the button (called the cutoff seat). You smooth-call Al's bet. Novice Nancy just calls on the button. Both of the blinds fold. With three of you in the pot, $260 is sitting in the middle of the table.

The flop comes 6-6-Q. Al bets $200.

What's Your Move?

Analysis

Action Al is capable of raising with lots of different hands. You have flopped the nut flush draw with two overcards. As long as Al doesn't have aces or kings, this is a good flop for your hand.

The Strategy We Suggest

With the nut flush draw and two overcards, you have a very big hand. Move all in. Action Al may give it up and you can win it right on the flop. Or if he calls, you might make the hand that will beat him.

As you gain more experience, you might try this intermediate strategy: Smooth-call hoping to bring Novice Nancy into the pot. By smooth-calling in this spot, you will still have $700 left. And if Al doesn't have a big hand, he might check the turn. In that case, you could either make a semi-bluff for $300 to try to win the pot right there, or you could see all the cards for free by also checking.

SCENARIO 52

The flop:

You are sitting on the button with:

Before the flop Reckless Rick brings it in for $75. We are sitting on the button with A-Q suited and just call the raise. Novice Nancy folds in the small blind. Loose Louie calls in the big blind. The pot is now $235. The flop comes 6-6-Q. Loose Louie bets out $200 from the big blind. Rick thinks and then calls the $200. It's up to you.

What's Your Move?

Analysis

Even though Rick raised before the flop, we know from our observations of his play that he is capable of raising with any type of hand. We can always count on Louie to defend his blind with almost any two cards. We have flopped top pair with top kicker, giving us two pair on the flop.

Before we decide whether to raise, call or fold, let's

analyze what hands Louie or Rick could be playing against us. Because Rick has called Louie's $200 bet on the flop, we now have some additional information about the possible strength of his hand. If he had a queen or an overpair, Reckless Rick probably would have raised Louie's bet on the flop, so we put him on a middle to low pair, or two overcards. But there's a danger: Because of the unpredictable cards that he raises with, Reckless Rick could have something like an A-6 suited—in which case, he would just flat-call Louie's flop bet in order to set a trap for him (and us, if we call) on the turn.

Let's think about what Loose Louie might have that he was so proud of to call a raise with before the flop, and then to lead with on the flop. Since Louie leads at the pot, it more likely that he has a queen than a six in his hand. If you just call, you would not get any additional information about the strength of your opponents' hands. If you raise, there's a good chance that Reckless Rick will fold.

But what about Loose Louie? If he has a six in his hand, he'll come back over the top of you.

The Strategy We Suggest

Raise. There now is $635 in the pot—$235 before the flop, Louie's $200 bet, and Rick's $200 call. You have $925 in chips. We suggest that you raise it to $500. As a beginning player, you probably cannot get away from this hand. Even if Louie and/or Rick comes back over the top of you for all your chips, you'll have to go with the hand. And of course, you might even have the best hand. Judging on their play in previous hands, you know that either of them might have a worse hand than you do. For example, Louie could have a queen with a worse kicker than yours.

SCENARIO 53

The flop:

We are sitting in the big blind holding the trash hand:

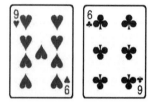

Before the flop, Tight Ted limps from first position, Novice Nancy limps in behind him, and Action Al limps on the button. Authority Artie calls from the small blind and we check in the big blind. There is $125 in the pot before the flop. The flop comes 6-6-Q. Artie checks.

What's Your Move?

Analysis

Naturally we're going to play this hand. The big question is what is the best way to get the most money into the pot. We realize that there are inherent dangers in the hand. One more six is out—and that's really the only thing we have to worry about unless one of our opponents (most likely Tight Ted, if anybody) limped with pocket queens.

We can pretty well figure that Ted does not have a six in his hand.

The Strategy We Suggest

Check, hoping to check-raise. Since we have Action Al on the button, we can safely predict that he's going to bet with anything if it's passed to him. Our check also will give us additional information about Tight Ted's hand. Our best scenario is to trap two or even three of our opponents into betting with either a queen or an overpair. (Wouldn't it be nice if three of them each had a queen, leaving them all drawing dead to our trip sixes? How much sweeter can it get?)

Flop Six

Three Middle Connectors/Unsuited

The flop:

SCENARIO 54

The flop:

We are sitting in middle position and look down at:

Before the flop, everybody passed to us and we brought it in for $100. We didn't raise just three times the big blind, we made a slightly larger raise to discourage anybody from calling behind us with hands such as K-Q or even Q-10 or a weak ace (A-9 or A-x). Novice Nancy called in the cutoff seat, Tight Ted folded in the small blind, and Action Al called in the big blind. The pot size is $310.

On the flop, Action Al bets $250.

What's Your Move?

Analysis

Because the flop came with small cards, players like Action Al often think that the raiser has missed the flop and lead at it. What kinds of hands might Al have? He could have flopped a pair, or a straight draw, or nothing. The chances that he flopped a straight are slim to none, because he probably would have checked if he hit the straight on the flop, hoping that you would bet it for him.

Novice Nancy could have any big-card hand such as A-K, A-Q, K-Q, or maybe a pocket pair. Unless Nancy has flopped a set, our overpair probably is the best hand on the flop.

The Strategy We Suggest

In answer to Al's $250 bet, we suggest moving all in. If you raise double his bet ($500), you will have only $400 left in a situation in which you are pot-logged to start with. If they do have a straight draw, they'll have to pay dearly to draw to it. You might just as well put your opponents to the test right here on the flop and possibly pick up a $460 profit.

SCENARIO 55

The flop:

You are sitting in late position with:

Before the flop, Tight Ted limped in for $25 and everyone else folded to you. You raised to $100, the small blind threw away his cards, and Reckless Rick called from the big blind. Tight Ted also called the raise. The pot size is $310 before the flop. On the flop, both Rick and Ted check.

What's Your Move?

Analysis

This is not a good flop for Big Slick. It is dangerous because it is connected. You don't put Tight Ted on a big hand because, if he had aces, kings or queens, he probably would have reraised before the flop. And you don't think he has a set.

Why?

Because this is a dangerous flop for a set (with its possible straight draws), so Ted most likely would lead at the flop to discourage anybody from calling and possibly outdrawing him if he had flopped a set. You figure that Ted is out of the picture now, so the only opponent you need to worry about is Reckless Rick. Of course if he had hit anything at all on the flop, he probably would have bet it.

The Strategy We Suggest
Bluff at the pot with a $200 bet. It's fun to win with no pair! If either opponent raises you, fold. If either or both of them calls, just check it through unless you hit a pair on the turn.

SCENARIO 56

The flop:

You are sitting in the big blind in an unraised pot with:

Passive Paul and Solid Sam limped into the pot before the flop and Authority Artie called in the little blind.

On the flop, Artie leads out for $100 from the small blind.

What's Your Move?

Analysis

You have flopped an open-end straight draw with an over card. Your perfect card to catch would be a ten, which would give you a jack-high straight. This is good because if someone else has a nine and a ten comes off, you will bust them with your superior straight, an occurrence that would make you a very happy camper.

Solid Sam, who limped in behind us, could have limped with pocket aces, kings, or some other pair in order to set a trap. Because of his style of play, it is hard to guess whether he's slow-playing a big hand before the flop, or whether he's just trying to see a cheap flop. Passive Paul also could have anything—he never learned the old axiom, "A bettor be, a caller never." He is a calling station.

There's a good chance that Authority Artie has a pair, or possibly even a pair with a straight draw—a hand like 9-8, 9-9, 5-5. He could even have a 5-4 suited to make the low end (the "ignorant" end) of the straight on the flop. If that is true, he would be more likely to bet on the flop than if he had 10-9 and flopped the nuts

The Strategy We Suggest
Smooth-call Artie's $100 opening bet.

SCENARIO 57

The flop:

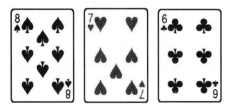

You are sitting in middle position with:

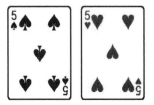

Before the flop, Passive Paul limped in front of us. We just called from middle position, and everybody folded to Authority Artie in the big blind, who just checked. With three of us in the hand before the flop, the pot has $85 in it. On the flop, Artie and Paul both check to you.

What's Your Move?

Analysis

The 8-7-6 flop gives us a draw to the low end of the straight with lots of danger lurking in the shadows. For example, if a nine comes on the turn giving us a 9-high straight, it also could give an opponent the 10-high straight. A four is the only straight card that would give us any confidence that we have the best hand—and even then we wouldn't want to risk a lot of money betting the hand. Since everyone limped before the flop, it is quite possible that one of our opponents has a 10-9 and has been slow-playing his straight from the get-go.

The Strategy We Suggest

Also check. Then hope for a four on the turn card when nobody else has a higher straight—or even better, runner-runner fives!

Flop Seven

A High Pair with a Low Card

The flop:

SCENARIO 58

The flop:

Before the flop, Novice Nancy limped in first position for $25. Everyone passed to us in middle position. Your hand is:

You raised to $100 and everyone folded around to Loose Louie in the big blind. Louie called the raise and so did Nancy, bringing the pot to $310. On the flop, Louie bets $150 and Nancy calls. Now it's up to you.

What's Your Move?

Analysis

You have flopped an overpair to the flop. Normally, your overpair might be the best hand, and you have position on your two opponents (you are last to act on the hand). You know that Loose Louie is capable of betting in an effort to represent a jack in his hand—he would like to steal the pot.

In contrast, Nancy doesn't really understand the strength of her hands. When she calls Al's bet on the flop, you suspect that she has something—either a pocket pair or possibly a jack. You want to try to find out where you are.

The Strategy We Suggest

Raise to $400. If one of them reraises, throw your queens away. It would be very hard for them to raise you back in this situation if they couldn't beat your queens. If either of them calls—or especially if they both call—play very carefully from then onward. For example, if they call your raise on the flop and then check the turn, you would also check and wait to see what they do on the river.

At this point everyone left in the pot would have half their chips in the pot ($500) with $500 left in their stack. In other words, everyone in the hand is under the pressure of going broke.

SCENARIO 59

The flop:

You are sitting in a middle position with:

Before the flop, Solid Sam limped in first position for $25, we also limped from middle position, and Reckless Rick called from the button. Both blinds also came into the pot, which now has $125 in it.

On the flop, the two blinds and Solid Sam check to you.

What's Your Move?

Analysis

You have flopped a very big hand. You are thinking, "Please let someone bet or, better yet, move in on me!" because you want to get as much money into this pot as you can. There aren't many draws to be afraid of—the only hands you are a dog to at this time are 7-7 or J-7. If there is a J-7 out against you, it most likely would be in one of the blind hands.

You also have Reckless Rick, who likes to put chips in the pot, waiting to act behind you.

The Strategy We Suggest

Check. Give Rick a chance to bet behind you on the button. Your hand is big enough that you can afford to let the turn card come off. If someone draws out on you, too bad—you were just trying to win a lot of chips with a premium hand and there's no harm in that.

SCENARIO 60

The flop:

You are sitting under the gun with:

Before the flop, you raised to $100 under the gun. Sitting to your immediate left, Tight Ted called. Novice Nancy called on the button and Action Al called from the big blind. With four players in action, the pot size was $410 before the flop. On the flop, Action Al bets $200 from the big blind. Now it's your turn to act.

What's Your Move?

Analysis

Your hand was a raising hand before the flop. You didn't like seeing Tight Ted come into the pot because you know that he has a hand good enough to justify calling your pre-flop raise. The good news is that he didn't reraise, meaning that he probably doesn't have a big pair. Of course just calling doesn't mean for sure that he doesn't have a big pair.

Good players are capable of making a deceptive play in which they flat-call a raise with a big pair in the hope of luring other players into the pot. The flop wasn't what you were looking for, although the good news is that you have two overcards.

The bad news is that if you hit an ace and someone has an A-J, you will be in big trouble.

The Strategy We Suggest

Fold. Ooops! We missed the flop. When Al bets in front of you, he could be pushing you into the fire if you call. Even if he doesn't have you beaten, Ted or Nancy probably does.

Save the chips for another hand.

SCENARIO 61

The flop:

You are in the $25 big blind holding:

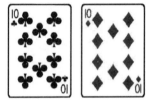

Before the flop, everyone folded to Action Al on the button. Al raised to $75 and the little blind folded. You called. On the J-J-7 flop, you are first to act.

What's Your Move?

Analysis

You know that Action Al likes to mix it up. He enjoys stealing blinds and doesn't have to have a big hand to try it. Your pocket tens is an underpair to the flop, but still could be the best hand. From Al's point of view, which play could you make that would make your hand look the strongest to him?

Should you bet at the pot, or should you try for a check-raise?

If you check, there's a good chance that Al will bet,

setting up the check-raise. If you check and he checks behind you, a warning light should go on in your head. What kind of hand would he check with? You must suspect that he has a jack.

The Strategy We Suggest

Check to Al. If he bets between $100-$150, for example, raise him about one and a half times what he bet (a $150-$225 raise). If he plays back at you (he reraises), throw your tens away. If Al checks after you check, continue to check the flop and river because you suspect that he could be slow-playing a jack.

If you think things through, you can see the kinds of head games that often are played between opponents. You will understand them better the more advanced you get.

PART TEN

Bluffing Practice Hands

SCENARIO 62

THE SEMI-BLUFF

You are in the early stages of a tournament with the blinds at $25-$50. Passive Paul and Tight Ted both limp in for $50.

You are on the button with:

You also limp. Novice Nancy in the small blind calls the extra $25, and Reckless Rick in the big blind checks.

The flop comes:

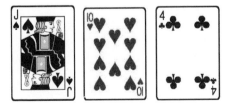

You have an open-end straight draw and two overcards. The action is checked around to you.

What's Your Move?
A. Check
B. Bet about $200

Analysis
We know that if either Reckless Rick or Tight Ted had a jack in his hand, he would bet. Passive Paul and Novice Nancy could have anything, but they probably don't have a jack or they would most likely have bet.

The Strategy We Suggest
This is a good chance to try to pick up the pot with a bet (B). If you get called, you can still improve to a nut straight or pair up and possibly make the best hand. You are betting without a made hand, but you have a hand that could easily improve to the best hand in case you get called. Much of the time you will win because everybody will fold when you bet.

SCENARIO 63

THE SEMI-BLUFF

You hold:

You are in early position and bring it in for a standard raise of three times the size of the big blind.

The blinds are $25 and $50 and everyone has about $1,000 in chips. Passive Paul and Loose Louie call the raise, and the blinds fold.

The flop looks like this:

You have flopped a royal flush draw!

What's Your Move?

A. Check and call if somebody bets.

B. Check and fold if somebody bets—all you have is a draw and you can't even beat a pair

C. Make about a pot sized bet

Analysis

Although you do not have a made hand, you do have a monster draw. You know that a flop containing two cards that are ten or higher could have improved somebody's hand, but this is a hand you want to gamble with. You figure that Paul will call if he makes top pair, but is likely to fold anything less than that. If he has a flush or open-end straight draw, Paul may call on the flop and pass on fourth street if he doesn't improve.

Louie loves to play middle connecting cards and would likely have reraised with a big pair or even A-Q.

The Strategy We Suggest

Knowing the types of cards that Louie and Paul play, a bet (C) is in order here. You are most likely going to play this hand to the river, and you don't mind winning it with a bet on the flop.

SCENARIO 64

THE STEAL BLUFF

It is late in the tournament with twenty players left at three shorthanded tables. The tournament pays eighteen places. You are one of the top three chip leaders with $25,000 in chips. The other players at your table have mostly short and medium stacks. The blinds are now $400-$800 and your opponents are playing tight, in the hope that they can make it into the money. One of the medium stacks is in the big blind and a fairly short stack is in the small blind.

Everyone has passed to you sitting in the cutoff seat (one seat in front of the button). You look down to find:

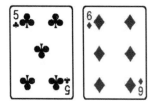

What's Your Move?
    A. Call the $800 big blind
    B. Fold
    C. Raise to about $3,000

Analysis
All you have is a six-high hand, but you know that the big blind will not call a large raise unless he has a premium hand. The short stack in the small blind is likely to fold in order to give himself another entire round to

find a good hand to put his money in with. Even if he does have a strong enough hand to call you, you might still get lucky and out-flop him.

The Strategy We Suggest

You know that the short stack can't hurt you too much even if he calls your raise and wins the pot. With little to risk, this is a good time to try to steal the blinds (C).

THE STEAL BLUFF - 2

You are in the middle stage of the tournament with a $50 ante and blinds of $200-$400. You have a below average stack of about $2,600 in chips. There is $1,100 in the pot before the cards are dealt. You are two seats away from the button. You have a tight image at the table. Everyone has folded so far.

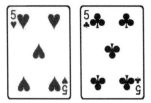

Your hand is pocket fives, a hand that is very vulnerable to both overcards and a bigger pair.

What's Your Move?
A. Fold and wait for a better hand

B. Call the minimum bet and hope to hit a set on the flop

C. Make a standard raise of three to four times the size of the big blind

D. Move all in

Analysis
With a tight table image, it is easier for you to attempt to pick up the blinds and antes without a premium hand. You are in late position with a small pair, a hand that may be good at the moment but which can easily get beaten if

you don't flop a five. If you make a standard raise, about half of your chips would be committed to the pot, and if somebody else raises behind you, you would most likely call.

The Strategy We Suggest

Moving in (D) is the best play in this situation. You still have enough chips to make a sizeable raise. Further, nobody can attempt to steal the pot from you after the flop if all your chips are already in the pot.

THE RESTEAL BLUFF

Suppose you are playing in a tournament where the blinds are $100-$200 and the ante is $25. You have been at this table since the $25-$50 round. You are the big blind. On your immediate right in the small blind is Tight Ted and to his right, sitting on the button, is Reckless Rick, who seems to raise every time he has the button. Unfortunately, even though you know that he can't have a hand every time he's on the button, you have never held a hand when he has raised.

Because you've been running cold and haven't caught any premium cards, your chips have continually eroded to the point that you only have a total of $2,600 in chips, with $200 in the big blind.

Everyone folds to Rick on the button, who has about $3,000—sure enough, he raises to $600. Tight Ted folds. You're begging, "Please let me find a hand to play against him."

But you look down to find this:

What's Your Move?
A. Fold
B. Call
C. Move all in

Analysis
When a very aggressive player continually puts on the pressure by raising whenever he has the button, you know that he probably doesn't have a hand every time. Your hand isn't very strong, but since you have a good table image, your opponents should give you respect when you raise or reraise.

The Strategy We Suggest
This is a good spot to bluff, so we suggest moving all-in on Rick (C). By trying the resteal bluff, you're taking a calculated gamble that he doesn't have a hand that he can call your all-in raise with. If he does call, maybe you'll get lucky.

SCENARIO 67

THE RESTEAL BLUFF - 2

Now suppose the blinds are $300-$600 with a $50 ante. You are in the small blind with $5,000 in chips. Everyone folds around to you.

You look down to find:

Action Al is in the big blind with $7,000 in chips.

What's Your Move?
    A. Move all in
    B. Call $300
    C. Raise to $1,800
    D. Fold

Analysis
You don't have a very big hand with A-10 offsuit and you're getting short on chips. Action Al, who does lots of raising— especially when he senses weakness—is sitting behind you.

If you move in here, he will only call if he has a better hand than you do.

The Strategy We Suggest

You would like to improve your chip position, so we suggest calling the extra $300 that is required to complete the bet (B). After you call, it is possible that Al will make a normal raise to $1,800. If he does, move in on him to try to bluff him out of the pot by attempting a resteal (A). Against his raise, moving all in is the best play because Al will need a very strong hand to call your move-in reraise.

THE FOLLOW-UP BLUFF

You are in the middle stages of the tournament with an average stack of $2,000 in chips. The blinds are now $50- $100. You are in the cutoff seat. Solid Sam is on the button, one seat to your left. Passive Paul is in the small blind and Tight Ted is in the big blind. You think this might be a good opportunity to pick up the blinds, so you make it $350 to go.

Sam thinks for a few seconds and then folds. Passive Paul folds and Tight Ted decides to call.

You have:

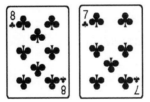

The flop comes:

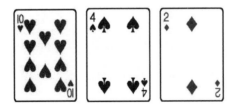

Ted checks and you try to steal the pot by betting $500. Ted calls. The turn card is the K♦. Ted checks again.

The action is up to you.

What's Your Move?
A. Check

B. Move all-in

Analysis
There was no logical draw on the flop. When Ted called your bet on the flop, he most likely had a ten in his hand or some kind of pocket pair.

What you fear the most is that Ted flopped a set and is slow-playing it. You have no chance to win this pot by checking. You know that Ted does not call the flop with just overcards, so the king on the turn is a scare card for him if he does indeed have an A-10.

The Strategy We Suggest
This is a good opportunity to try a follow-up bluff. This is a good time to move all in (B) and steal the pot from him.

After all, we call him "Tight" Ted for a reason.

THE FOLLOW-UP BLUFF - 2

It is the early stage of the tournament. Two players have limped into the pot.

You are on the button with:

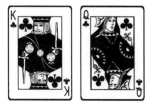

You also limp in. Both blinds see the flop "cheap." That is, the small blind completes the minimum bet and the big blind just calls.

The flop is:

Everyone checks to you. Trying to steal, you decide to bet $125, the size of the pot. Both blinds fold, as does the first limper. Authority Artie stalls for about a minute and then finally decides to call, asking "Do you really have an ace?"

The turn card is another ace. Artie checks.

What's Your Move?
A. Check
B. Bet around $300
C. Move all in

Analysis
Since Artie was the next to last to act, it is almost certain that he does not have an ace in his hand because he didn't bet. He probably has either a seven in his hand or a pocket pair. Artie prides himself on his ability to read other players. He will make an occasional great call, and will make what he thinks is a good fold if he thinks he is beaten.

The Strategy We Suggest
If Artie thinks you have an ace, he knows that he probably is drawing dead. If you check, you can't win in a showdown. If you move in and overbet the pot, Artie might suspect a bluff and call you. The right play is (B). When you make a bet that is less than the size of the pot, it looks as though you want some action.

You're counting on Artie to think this through and decide to fold.

SCENARIO 70

THE TOTAL BLUFF

You are in the late stage of the tournament with a medium stack. The blinds are $300-$600 with a $50 ante. You have about $12,000 in chips. Novice Nancy, who has about the same amount of chips, limps in under the gun for $600. Passive Paul also limps in from middle position.

You are sitting in the cutoff seat with:

You raise it to $2,800. Nancy thinks for a minute and then decides to fold. Paul thinks for awhile and then reluctantly calls. You are putting Paul on a mid-range pair, probably tens or nines. Paul has about $14,000 in chips, slightly more than you.

The flop comes:

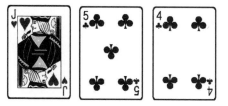

Paul checks. You decide to try to steal the pot by betting $4,000. Paul hesitates some more and finally calls. The 7♦ comes on the turn card, apparently helping nobody. Paul checks and you check. The river card is the Q♣. Paul checks again.

What's Your Move?

A. Check because we know we can't beat Paul's pair

B. Move all in

Analysis

You know that you cannot win a showdown with just an ace-high hand. You already have over half of your chips in the pot, but you still have enough to make a large bet. The Q♣ is another overcard to the pair that you think Paul is holding, plus it is a flush card. This has to be a very scary river card for Paul.

You played the hand as though you either had two big cards in your hand or a flush draw. You didn't make either of those hands, of course, but you would love to have those chips in the middle of the table. They would help your chip position a whole lot.

The Strategy We Suggest

If you just check, you don't think that you can win in a showdown. Paul knows that if he calls and loses, he will be crippled. Your best shot to win this pot—and you want it badly—is to try a total bluff (B), all the while begging the poker gods, "Please let Paul fold."

SCENARIO 71

THE TOTAL BLUFF - 2

It is late in the tournament and you have a short stack of $5,000 in chips. The blinds are $300-$600 with a $75 ante. That puts $1,575 in the pot before the cards are dealt. The limits are going to increase in a few more hands, so this is the last time you will take the blinds before they increase. Passive Paul is in the small blind and you are in the big blind. Everyone folds to Paul, who calls the additional $300 to complete the bet.

After posting the blinds and the ante, you have $4,325 left in your stack. There is $1,875 in the pot after Paul's call. You look down at your hand and find a "monster" hand—the 7♣ 2♥—the worst starting hand in hold'em!

What's Your Move?
A. Check and hope for a miracle flop
B. Move all in

Analysis
You know that Passive Paul does not have a strong hand or he would have raised your short stack. If you check, you will need a miracle flop to play the hand. If you lose this pot and go through the small blind without

winning, you will have less than $4,000 in chips. "If I move in, will Paul call?" you ask yourself. The answer is no. Why? Because if he had a hand good enough to call your all-in raise with, Paul would have raised instead of just calling before the flop.

The Strategy We Suggest

This is the time to take a chance (B) and move all in. Even if Paul calls, sometimes you get very lucky and win. There is a very good chance that Paul will fold because you still have enough chips to make one sizeable raise. The strength of your hand—or the lack of strength—does not matter in this scenario. You are on a total bluff, betting that Paul will fold his hand.

PART ELEVEN

How to Play No-Limit Hold'em Cash Games in Online Casinos

Until recently, if you wanted to play no-limit hold'em, you had to play it in tournament mode because very few cardrooms spread no-limit hold'em cash games. One reason why on-land casinos don't usually spread no-limit cash games is that the house may be fearful that its regular players will go broke in no-limit play and the casino will lose them as customers.

In fact no-limit tournaments are more feasible than cash games for most of us to play because we put only a predetermined bankroll at risk in tournaments. We know in advance how much we can lose (the buy-in) and how much we can win (the top prize), which may give us a sense of security.

In today's expanding poker world, many online casinos and a few on-land cardrooms are filling the gap in opportunities to play no-limit hold'em cash games rather than offering tournament play only. Some online sites offer no-limit hold'em cash games with blinds as small as 5 cents-10 cents, and a few are even offering "play" money games in which you can practice your skills for a zero buy-in.

Play-money games are good places to get your feet

wet in a game that is new to you. They allow you to acquire a feel for how things work without taking any monetary risk. Just keep in mind that people play differently when they're just playing for fun and have no money at risk. Naturally, it is much more fun to play a lot of hands rather than sitting out of most of them. Therefore, expect to see lots of players in every hand when you play in a play-money game. Just remember that when you're ready to start playing for real money, you will need to tighten up your strategy.

In online cash games, the online site puts a maximum on the amount of money with which you can buy into a no-limit hold'em game. That way, players cannot put their entire bankroll on the table at one time, unless their bankroll is less than the maximum allowed buy-in.

We strongly suggest that you always play in a game that you can afford, one with blinds at which you feel comfortable playing. For example, if you feel more comfortable playing in a game with blinds of 25 cents- 50 cents than one with $1-$2 blinds, play the smaller game. Online casinos currently offer games with blinds as high as $3-$6. When you have mastered the smallest games, you can gradually move up to the higher games.

Now pull up a chair and buy into our virtual no-limit hold'em cash game and play along with Brad as he shows you the ropes. But before the deal begins, here are some pointers on playing these small games.

Here are some other things to remember when you start playing cash games:

• The blinds in cash games remain the same throughout the game. They do not increase at regular intervals, as the blinds do in tournaments.

• You are not playing against the clock, as you must do in tournaments. Therefore, you are never pressured into playing inferior hands just because the blinds are rising or you are very low on chips. Actually, playing cash games is good practice for playing the early rounds of a tournament when you have plenty of chips to play and no pressure.

• Unlike tournaments, you can quit playing at any time you choose.

• If you go broke, you can make another buy-in. You don't have to leave the game unless you have no more money in your online account.

Concentrate on These Factors

When you first begin playing no-limit hold'em, concentrate more on table position and strong starting-hand values. Pay careful attention to your seating position at the virtual table, and your position in the betting sequence. Always be aware of the types of players who have bet in front of you, and the types of player who can act after you.

Carefully Select the Hands You Play

Be very careful about hand selection. The hands that you play are determined by your position at the table, the action in front of you, the potential action from players sitting behind you, and the quality of your cards. As you get more mileage under your belt, you can expand the number of hands you play to include a few speculative hands. With experience, you will become more knowledgeable as to when to play them. Until that time, stick with strong starting hands only.

Practice Reading the Flop

While in these small cash games, continually practice reading the flop even when you aren't in the pot. Continually ask yourself, "If I were playing this hand, which two cards would I most like to be holding?" Then try to decide which player might have those cards. Also ask, "With the cards on this board, what is the best possible hand that could be made?"

Set a Loss Limit

We recommend that you set a loss limit when you first start playing no limit hold'em online. You should never lose more in one session than you can reasonably expect to win in the next session you play. For example, if you are playing with $2-$4 blinds and you lose around 100 times the size of the big blind, which in this case would be $400, it's time to quit. That should be your guideline for each game—lose no more than 100 times the big blind.

Know When to Quit the Game

"If I'm winning, when should I quit?" you might ask. That is a good question that each of us should always have in the back of our minds. If losing 100 times the size of the big blind should make us quit, how about winning 100 times the size of the big blind? The answer is—it depends. It depends on how good the game still is. Are the weak players still in the game and losing? Are you playing your A-game? How tired are you? How important to you is the money that you have just won? Only you can answer these questions. The best idea is to limit your loss, but do not limit your win.

Have Enough Money in Your Account

Put enough money in your online account to buy more chips if you need or want to. You need to have an adequate amount of money to back up your play. Playing on short or "scared" money is a surefire way to lose.

Take Advantage of Your Table Image

Your image at the table is also important. Do you think the other players see you as a loose or a tight player? Take advantage of whatever image you have created.

Let's look at some specific scenarios in our cash game and talk about how you might play your cards in different situations.

SCENARIO 72

Suppose this is your first time to play online. You have chosen a $1-$2 blind no-limit hold'em game that is in progress and buy in for $100. Before you are dealt any cards, the computer dealer flashes a message: "Do you want to post the $2 big blind, or wait for the big blind?"

What are your options? You can post the blind immediately, or you can wait until you are actually in the position of the big blind, or you can wait a few hands and then come in behind the dealer where you will have the best position. You choose to wait for the big blind.

After you reach the position of the big blind, you click "Post the big blind." You are dealt the:

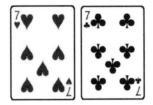

The player in first position raises the pot to $5. Everybody folds to the player on the button. The button calls. The small blind also calls. It's up to you.

What's Your Move?

Analysis

You are in the big blind with a pair of sevens, which is not a premium hand. But if you hit trips on the flop, you would be happy. Since no one can reraise if you just call, you call the raise in the hope of hitting the flop and winning a good pot. Notice that you play the same way in this situation as you would play in a tournament.

SCENARIO 73

Now suppose it's an hour later and you are playing in the same cash game. You have only $25 left with $2 in the big blind.

Your hand is the:

Five players limped into the pot, including the button and the small blind. The pot now has $12 in it. You check. The flop comes with the:

The small blind checks, you check, and Action Al, sitting to your left, bets $12. Everyone else calls the bet. With all the action on the flop, the pot now has $72 in it. You have $20 left.

What's Your Move?

Analysis

You have flopped the nut flush draw with five other players in the pot. If you call, you will only have $8 left. This is a good opportunity to gamble.

Our suggested play is to raise the rest of your chips—go all-in—in the hope of making the flush and winning a good pot. If you don't win, you can buy more chips.

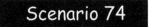

Scenario 74

Now suppose you make the flush that you were drawing to in Scenario 2 and you win the pot. You now have $132. Since you were in the big blind on the last hand, you are now in the small blind and must post $1. Tight Ted is the big blind and posts $2. Action Al, who has about $65 in chips, opens the pot for $8 under the gun (first position).

Everyone folds to Loose Louie, who is sitting on the button with about $200 in chips. Louie calls the $8.

You look at your hole cards and find:

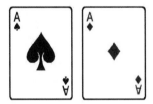

"Wow, I'm on a rush!" you're thinking.

What's Your Move?

Analysis

You're in a great spot—two action players are already in the pot. But before you act, ask yourself, "How can I get the most money into the pot before the flop?" Al, who just lost the last pot when you made the flush, now has $8 of his $65 in the pot. He might have his nose open, meaning that after just losing a big pot, he probably can't wait to fire in his chips to try to win some money back.

We suggest raising to about $25 to give Al enough room to move all in. If he reraises, he might even lure

Loose Louie into the pot. That way, you will get the action you are looking for with pocket aces.

Tom McEvoy, the 1983 World Champion of Poker, is the Poker Professor. Visit McEvoy at *www.PokerProfessor.com*, a site that provides expert answers to your poker questions.

PART TWELVE

10 Ways to Practice No-Limit Texas Hold'em

To get some practice at no-limit Texas hold'em before you venture into a live casino to play a big buy-in tournament, you can do what Tom and I did when we started playing poker—just get a group of friends together and have a home poker game. Or you can take advantage of the many opportunities for practice that are available to you in the modern world of poker. In this section we offer you our suggestions on ways to hone your no-limit hold'em skills.

You can practice in the convenience of your own home on the Internet via online casinos. The online casinos have everything from "play money" games where you play for free to real cash games that start at about 5-cent and 10-cent blinds up to much more expensive games. You can start at the level you feel comfortable and then move up as your skill improves.

Online casinos also sponsor multi-table tournaments, single-table tournaments, and satellites in which you can play for low buy-ins up to high buy-ins. Online tournaments and satellites are a great place to begin your no-limit hold'em practice, and you can find a tournament or satellite to play at almost any hour of the day and night.

Don't miss any chances to watch all the pros play on

television. Now that the players are showing their hands to the television audience, you can learn a lot about the way the cream of the crop play no-limit hold'em for big money.

If you live close to a casino that sponsors big or small tournaments, go and watch players in live action. While you are sitting in the audience, try figuring out what hands the players have and why they bet their hands the way they do.

Above all, have lots of fun and practice, practice, practice.

PRACTICE OPPORTUNITY #1:

Watch No-Limit Hold'em Televised Tournaments

Observing how players bet and play their hands during televised tournaments can help you get on the fast track of moving from a beginner to a winner in the world's most exciting and lucrative poker game, no-limit Texas hold'em.

A World Poker Tour tournament or the World Series of Poker might have started with 300 or more players, but you're seeing only the top few survivors on your television screen. When you watch a World Poker Tour tournament on TV, you see only the top six finalists playing at the championship table. The World Series of Poker starts filming when the final nine players have been determined.

The WPT has tournaments in various places all over the world. The WSOP is played in Las Vegas. The buy-in is usually between $5,000 and $25,000 in the WPT events and it is $10,000 for the WSOP championship tournament. The qualifications to enter usually are just being of age and posting the required buy-in. The tournament begins with many tables, usually with nine players per table. For example, if there are 270 players there would be thirty tables at the beginning of the tournament. In a $10,000 buy in event, everyone usually starts with $10,000 in chips.

In televised tournaments, most of the action happens before the flop and on the flop. When you see the players' hole cards on TV, you might notice that sometimes they bet with garbage hands. Other times they have very good hands. With so few players left in action, it's often "raise and take it," no matter what kind of hand the raiser has.

That is, whoever raises first often takes the pot.

And there's a lot of bluffing, which makes the game exciting for the audience as well as the players. Making a big bluff will test your nerves. It can even make your heart race, cause perspiration to pop out on your forehead, and induce heavy breathing. It is fun to make a successful bluff and win a pot just by pure guts—just watch the winners do it on TV and you'll see what I mean.

When you're playing or just watching, practice reading the board cards and determining what the best possible hand is with each new board card that is dealt. You should always be asking yourself, "What, at this moment, is the nuts?" It is impossible, for example, for anyone to have a full house or four of a kind unless the board is paired. But if someone has made the nut straight or the nut flush, you know that's the best possible hand because it is unbeatable at that point. However, things can change with every new card that comes out in the middle.

For example, if you start off with two aces in your hand, you have the nuts before the flop. Then, depending on the cards that come out on the board, the value of your cards may change. Suppose you have the Q♠ Q♣ and the flop comes with the Q♥ 2♣ 7♦. This is a great flop for your hand because you have a set of queens with no straight or flush draws possible. But if you had the Q♠ Q♣ and the flop came K♥ A♥ 10♥, that would be a horrible flop for your hand. Someone could have a flush, a straight, an ace or king in his hand to beat your two queens.

PRACTICE OPPORTUNITY #2:

Watch the Pros Play a Tournament in an On-Land Casino

One of the ways to sharpen your no-limit skills is to attend a major tournament in person and observe. At all of the World Poker Tour championship events, the best poker players on the planet compete for the gold and the glory, plus a chance to appear on television. Observing how these top players compete against each other can give you insights into some of the finer points of the game.

There is no greater thrill in poker than playing in the championship event of a major tournament—except for winning it, of course. Excitement permeates the air just before the first hand is dealt—players and observers alike can feel the electricity. Anybody who is at least twenty-one years old can compete in a poker tournament if he/she is willing to pony up the buy-in. Many fine amateur players join the competition and a lot of them, though not as renowned as the "name" players, are top players in their own right. You can also learn by observing these lesser-known players.

As an observer, what should you look for? If it is early in the competition, look for a table that has several well-known players and observe what they are doing in the early rounds. Often, they have very different styles of play, which makes it all the more interesting and educational. Try to read them. That is, think about what type of hand they might be betting, calling or raising with. At every stage of the competition, think about how you might have played the hand if you were sitting at the table.

The longer the tournament runs, the more exciting it

becomes. On days two or three, as the players get closer to the money spots and the final table, you can often feel the tension and see the concentration in their eyes. As the antes and blinds get higher, conservative play often goes out the window. Noticing when top players start making very aggressive plays can give you valuable strategy hints for your own future use.

The one disadvantage of watching a live tournament, as opposed to viewing a televised event, is that you do not get to see the players' hole cards unless the action goes to a showdown. Nevertheless, it can be rewarding and enlightening to see in person what it is like to compete at a high level. Further, since televised tournaments only concentrate on the final six players as a general rule, you will be able to note the strategy that top players use to make the final table. That is indeed worth observing and studying.

PRACTICE OPPORTUNITY #3:

Set Up a Home Tournament or Cash Game

A great way to practice your no-limit hold'em tournament skills is to set up a home game. Both Brad and I started our poker careers playing in home games, and believe me when I say that they can be both fun and profitable.

One way to set up a home game is to invite a few friends to play a one-table tournament. Even after I moved to Las Vegas to play poker professionally, I often had a tournament in my home to have some fun with friends on my birthday. One of them dubbed these annual affairs "The McEvoy Memorial Birthday Bash Tournament."

One possible structure for a home tournament is to charge everyone $20 and pay one or two places. If there is $200 in the prize pool, you could give 70 percent ($140) to the winner and 30 percent ($60) to the runner-up. You could also pay more places if you have more than ten players, or you could even make it a winner-take-all tournament.

I suggest starting everyone with $500 in chips and blinds of $10-$15. The blinds could go up every twenty or thirty minutes, with the next increase rising to $15-$30. After the $15-$30 level, take the $5 chips out of play and go to $25-$50 blinds, then $50-$100 and so on, until a winner has been crowned.

You could, of course, use any amount of chips you want and make the betting rounds longer. Usually, you want to have more than one tournament per night, so getting it over in a timely fashion will allow the losing players to get back in action without too long a wait.

You can even set up a home tournament using the World Series of Poker structure. You start with $10,000 in chips and $25-$50 blinds. Around the fourth or fifth level, you might also start using an ante, just like the WSOP and WPT events. If $20 is too little or, in some cases, too much to play for, adjust the buy-in to whatever the players are comfortable with.

If a tournament is not your cup of tea, then play no-limit hold'em as a cash game. I would suggest small blinds to start with, such as $1-$2 or less, with a maximum amount that each player can buy in for. You can also limit the amount of buy-ins permitted if a player goes broke. You want to keep the game friendly and interesting while making sure that nobody loses too much. A well-run game with clearly defined rules will keep players interested and wanting to play more.

PRACTICE OPPORTUNITY #4:

Play Small Buy-in Multi-Table Tournaments Online

Small buy-in online tournaments are available around the clock. Because of their almost unlimited availability, playing these small tournaments can greatly speed up your learning process. We adapted the material in this section from our book, *Championship Satellite Strategy*.

In the first levels you play solid, waiting for other people to make mistakes. Hopefully you can pick up a hand and double up in the first one or two rounds, or play a speculative hand cheaply. Because more chips are in play online, you can play a few more speculative hands in the early rounds without having it cost you too much.

You hope to strengthen your position a lot without hurting your chip position very much. This is particularly true in no-limit hold'em satellites where you have big implied odds. Starting with $1,500 in chips and fifteen minute rounds online, you have a fair amount of play and more opportunity to trap an opponent. In other words, if you limp in with weak hand, you're likely to get paid off very well (because of the implied odds) if you connect with the flop.

The blinds usually begin at $10-$20 and increase to $15-$30, $25-$50 and $50-$100. With cautious play and occasional mild speculation, you have an excellent chance of surviving through the break. You don't need to get out of line to double up. If you can pick up one hand and double up with it, you probably will have $3,000 in chips, which is about par with the average amount of chips once half the players are gone. That's a good spot to be in.

Usually about one-half of the starting field is eliminated during the first hour of play. Then you take a five minute break and when you return, the blinds increase to $75-$150. Then the blinds rise to $100-$200 for two rounds. At the beginning of the second round of $100-$200 blinds, you must start putting in an ante at many online casinos.

As the limits rise, you have to start opening up your hand requirements a little bit. "I've found that the key to survival is knowing when you're in trouble," Brad says. "When the limits rise to $100-$200, you're at the start of 'crunch' time. And when they rise to $200-$400, you are in the middle of crunch time." You are in trouble unless you have a par amount of chips, so you must accumulate chips. This is when you change your style of play from being very solid to being more aggressive.

Of course, aggressive play can pay off in any tournament you play, whether on-land or online. "If you don't have a strong right arm, if you aren't willing to push your chips in," Tom adds, "your chances of success are greatly reduced."

At the end of the first hour, about a half of the players are gone. By the time the blinds rise to $200-$400, only about twenty-five percent of the players are left. At the $200-$400 level, you need to have $4,000 to $5,000 in chips to feel secure. If you have any less than that, about five to six times the size of the big blind, you will be in a move-in mode any time you play a hand. When you're in that situation, there is a good argument to be made for just moving in rather than raising three to four times the size of the blind ($1,200-$1,600).

When you move in before the flop, your opponents know that you are committed to the end whereas, if you don't put in all your chips, they may think that you're not fully committed and might call with marginal hands. If they know you're committed to going all the way with the hand, they usually will fold those marginal hands, which is what you want them to do. Just winning the blinds is critically important at this stage. This move-in strategy applies to those times when you are shortstacked, not when you have a medium to large stack.

You cannot manufacture a good hand. It is the chip count and positional considerations that separate the men from the boys, so to speak. Making the right decisions about when to move, when to push the panic button, and when to be patient are important parts of the game. "One of the things I wrote in *Tournament Poker* is that you have to last long enough to give yourself a chance to get lucky," Tom explains. "Whoever wins a tournament has gotten lucky along the way. But you can't get lucky if you're no longer in it. You must develop good survival skills."

PRACTICE OPPORTUNITY #5:

Play Small-Stakes Rebuy Tournaments at On-Land Casinos

You can use most of the tournament strategies we just outlined when you play a low-limit, no-limit hold'em tournament in an on-land casino. In fact most small-stakes tournaments that are played in on-land casinos are rebuy events. Small buy-in tournaments sponsored by online casinos usually do not allow rebuys, although that is changing and some online sites these days do allow rebuys.

In a rebuy tournament, when you run out of money, you can put in more money and receive another stack of chips. This discussion of rebuy strategy has been adapted from *Poker Tournament Tips from the Pros* by Shane Smith.

The type of tournament you enter determines a major part of your playing strategy. In freeze-out events (those with no rebuys allowed), your primary concern in the early stages of play is making it to the next level in good shape. Therefore your strategy might be more conservative than it would be if you could buy more chips if you went broke.

Most low-stakes tournaments in on-land casinos are not freeze-outs—they allow multiple rebuys, either when you go broke or fall below a minimum chip count, plus an add-on at the end of the rebuy period. With so many opportunities to refill your monetary canteen at the rebuy oasis, your strategy will differ from freeze-out tournaments in which you cannot quench your thirst for chips except by winning them.

In most cases, you will need to take advantage of the rebuy and add-on options to be one of the top finishers.

Therefore when you enter a rebuy tournament, take enough money with you to cover two or three rebuys and the add-on. For example, if the entry fee is $20, plan to spend $40 to $60 on the tournament (one or two $10 rebuys and the $10 add-on). If you are on a limited bankroll, it may be better to save your funds for a live action game or for a freeze-out event because your insufficient bankroll can become a significant drawback in playing optimal rebuy tournament strategy.

When you go broke, it usually is correct to rebuy. If your winning expectation seems to be favorable—you feel confident that you can win and there will be a big pay-off—rebuy so long as you feel comfortable with the number of times you do so. Although I have seen players make an excessive number of rebuys, I believe that they probably should have accepted the decision of the poker gods who decided not to smile on them that day, and bow out of the fray. Remember that the main reason you're playing the tournament is to get a big return on a small investment.

Deciding whether to add on usually is determined by your chip status when the add-on option comes up. If you are low on chips, add on. If you are the chip leader, do not add on. And if you are in a middle chip position, add on.

Who has the chips may also be a factor in deciding whether to add on, particularly in small on-land tournaments (ten to thirty entrants) where you know most of the players. If you see that a very weak player who has been on a lucky streak holds one of the top chip positions, it probably is wise to take the add-on option so that you will have additional ammunition to use in taking advantage of his weak play. But if a strong player is top dog and you have a small stack, it probably will not increase your chances of a win enough to justify the add-on. If you are playing a tournament with a lot of entrants (more than fifty or so), most of whom you don't know, it is more difficult to determine the skill level of the players in top chip position. In that case, use your best judgement.

PRACTICE OPPORTUNITY #6:

Play One-Table Tournaments and Satellites Online

The structure of a typical one-table no-limit hold'em satellite has ten players starting with $800 to $1,000 in chips each. The blinds are usually $10-$15 in the first level of play. They rise to $15-$30 in the second round, and go up to $25-$50 in the third round, $50-$100 in the fourth round, and $100-$200 in the fifth round. The blinds rise to $150-$300 in the sixth round and so on through the rest of the tournament. While you are playing these one-table tournaments, use the betting charts on pages 60-61 as a guide for your betting strategy.

The strategy in this section is adapted from *Championship Satellite Strategy*.

The First Round

The relative strength of a starting hand changes depending on the number of players in the game. Because more people are playing against you when the game is ten-handed, you need a stronger starting hand than you would need when the game is five-handed, for example. A marginal hand that you would throw away when the game is ten-handed may become playable when the table is short. Also remember that when the game is ten-handed in the early stage of the satellite, there isn't much blind money in the pot to fight for, therefore you have less reason to try to steal pots with substandard hands.

Your position at the table is especially important in no-limit hold'em. Play more conservatively in early positions. In the first three positions after the blind, you definitely want to play only premium hands and usually bring it in for a raise when you enter the pot. You can play more liberally from middle to late position in unraised pots when two or three limpers are in the pot. You are looking for a situation where you can win a pot and maybe double up, all the while trying to avoid getting eliminated. Always remember that you cannot win the satellite during the first round of play, but you can lose it if you make a mistake.

Trouble hands can be even more trouble in no-limit hold'em than they are in limit hold'em. The blinds are very small in relation to the risks involved, so why get involved with a K-Q when someone raises in front of you? You could lose your whole stack with this trouble hand. You might want to slow-play in early position with pocket aces or pocket kings in the first round hoping that someone will raise and you can reraise him.

The Second Round

In the second level, the blinds usually go up to $10-$25. Things will be pretty much the same as the first level. You're seeing who's playing fast, who's tight, who's scared. You're also looking for people that you might be able to steal a pot from later on—as well as identifying players who might try to steal from you. Knowing these things, you can decide who to play with when somebody comes in for a raise, and can better judge what kinds of hands you want to play.

The Third Round

At the third level, usually about seven or eight players are left. The blinds rise to $25-$50, meaning that it costs you $75 per round to play. The normal raise is $150-$200. You want to continue playing conservatively in this level, all the while looking for an opportunity to double up with a premium hand.

The Fourth Round

The blinds are $50-$100. Now you have to pick up a few more pots because, with fewer players still in action, the blinds are coming around faster. Your goal is to preserve your chip position if you already have a lot of chips, or gain on the chip leaders if you're trailing. At the least, you want to survive and maintain your relative chips position.

Players now are playing more aggressively in order to pick up the blinds. Even the tighter players have to start opening up their game (playing looser) because of the larger blinds and the smaller field of players. From the fourth round onward, it is very important to know when your chips are in jeopardy, when you are committed to the pot, and when you need to improve your chip position by gathering some chips.

Stealing the blinds at this level becomes very important, and you're always trying to figure out who's out of line (playing a weak hand) when they try to steal your blind. You are reading your opponents and trying to figure out what they actually have. If you are fairly certain that you have the best hand and you think they're weak, you can try to make them lay down a hand by coming over the top of them (reraising, moving in) before the flop. You're not looking to see flops, you want to win it before the flop. In fact when you come over the top of someone, or raise trying to steal the blinds, remember that you are making a play in the hope of improving your chip position.

If you get broke in one of these plays—you run into a better hand or you get drawn out on—that is just a part of the game. In order to play no-limit hold'em well, you must make these plays when the time is right.

The Fifth Round of Play

The blinds are $100-$200. There usually are about five to six players left in action at this level. If at all possible, you don't want to let your chips get so low that it would be correct for your opponents to call any bet that you make. If you have only twice the size of the big blind, your opponents usually will call you with all sorts of marginal hands—and they usually are correct in doing so. Having four times the size of the big blind will give you a chance to pick up a pot.

If you are down to two or three times the size of the big blind and you have a truly hopeless hand like a 7-2 or 8-3, what do you do? In this scenario, if it is highly likely that your opponent will call you, you're better off waiting for the big blind. Now say that it's three-handed and you're in the big blind with chips (you're in either first or second place). Fred is the short stack and he desperately needs chips. He goes all in for $400, double your big blind. What do you do?

You call him in a heartbeat with any ace, any pair, any two cards ten or higher, any king-small—indeed you can call him with any reasonable two cards if you have the lead and his all-in bet is no more than double the big blind. Why? Because you have a chance to take him out of action. What if he only has $300 and goes all in? You can call him with "ATC," any two cards; essentially, you call him in the dark. You don't want to double him up, of course, but sometimes you have to take that risk. You gotta have heart, as the old song goes.

If you have three times the big blind, just calling is never correct at this level—there aren't any two cards that you just call with. If you play a hand, you're going for all your chips. You cannot be afraid to go broke. In no-limit hold'em, you just say to yourself, "I'm short, I've gotta get more chips, so I've just gotta make a stand." When you raise all in, you are simply making a calculated gamble that your opponents don't have a hand that they can call you with. You're trying to make the most of a bad situation.

You gamble more with a short stack than you do with a big stack. Why? Because you're forced to do it. You have to improve your chip position. When you're the short stack there's only one direction to go—up. You're already at the bottom and you want to get to the top. The only way to get chips is to fire. You're going to change your position one way or the other—you either go out the door or you get more chips.

Now, suppose you're lucky enough to be dealt a premium hand such as a big pair, A-K, A-Q, or even A-J. In this scenario you don't care who you go in against, although you might prefer going against the shorter stack (assuming that he calls your all-in raise) because if you win the pot, you will knock him out and will have equal chips to the big stack. Remember that when you start with twenty-five percent of the chips, you are only two pots away from winning the satellite.

The Sixth Round

The blinds are $150-$300. You usually are down to three player or less. There is no limping. You have to take at least a reasonable hand and go with it. You don't have much time to wait when you're playing three-handed. And when you start playing heads-up, it sometimes gets to the point where both you and your opponent know that you're pretty much going to go all in on the next hand.

Some Tips for Playing Heads-Up

You are usually heads-up with the blinds at $200-$400. The tournament becomes a blind-stealing event, strictly a move-in game. Even when you're still playing three-handed at these high blinds, one player steals, then the next player steals, and so on, until a player wakes up with a hand that he decides to play against an opponent that he thinks is trying to steal. In these types of situations, A-10 might look like a calling hand if you think that your opponent probably has a worse hand and is on a steal. You have to gamble more heads-up. You cannot allow yourself to get run over.

Now, suppose you are heads-up in the big blind and your opponent limps in from the small blind. With any hand that is better than the average random hand—any ace, any king, any pair—you probably will move in. Usually when an opponent limps in from the small blind in heads-up play, he has one of two types of hands: a strong hand that he's trying to trap you with, or a marginal had that he wants to see the flop with. Poker always requires making a judgment. Will my opponent call or won't he? If you firmly believe that he will fold, you can make a play at the pot, no matter what type of hand you have.

You're gambling all your chips that he won't call. The only type of hand he will call you with is a strong hand. The chances are better that he has nothing, so you are the favorite to pick up the pot.

Now, suppose you have pocket aces or kings. Would you limp or raise? Ask yourself, "How can I get the most money into this pot?" One option is to make a mini-raise, double the amount of the big blind. Or, if you're against a very aggressive player you might just limp with your big pocket pair. Why? Because you know that he probably will try to blow you out of the pot. By letting him raise, you will have him right where you want him. Use your best judgment when you have a big hand in heads-up play. Use whatever strategy you believe will be most effective in getting the maximum chips in the pot.

OPPORTUNITY #7:

Discuss Things with Knowledgeable Players

Sometimes, after you've played a difficult hand, you wonder, "Should I have played it differently?"

At times like this, it would be nice to have a poker guru with whom you could discuss your play. Your poker guru should be someone that you respect, a winning player who has plenty of experience, and is someone that you trust to give you good advice.

It is a huge asset to have someone you can trust to give you sound advice to improve your poker. When you ask a trusted advisor to help you, be prepared to give him all the details of the hand, including the type of game, the amount of the blinds and how soon they were going to rise, how much money you had, how much money your opponents had, what kind of players they were (tight, loose, aggressive, passive, scared), and what your table image was.

What kinds of questions do you want to ask your guru? You might ask whether any other playing options were possible, whether he would have played it differently, and how you might have increased your profit or decreased your loss in the play of the hand.

Through the years both Tom and I have been fortunate in making many close friends in the poker world. We have discussed the play of lots of hands, some with differences of opinions. These differences of opinion have helped me to adjust my strategies by seeing things from a different point of view.

In the late 1980s, we were down to the last table of a $1,000 buy in no-limit hold'em tournament at Amarillo Slim's Super Bowl of Poker. I was in middle chip position with around $10,000 in chips. The short stack in first position moved all-in for about $4,500. I looked down to find the K♠ K♦. I moved over the top of the raiser for all my chips. The player to my left, George Rodis, thought and thought, and finally folded. Everyone else folded, too, leaving only the short stack and me in the pot.

The flop came with the K♣ 9♥ 2♦. "I had an A-K," George said, sounding disturbed that he didn't call my raise. I won the pot with my trip kings, sending the short stack to the rail. In retrospect, I realized that if I hadn't reraised I also would have busted George and put myself in a commanding chip position to win the tournament. As it turned out, I ended up finishing up in fifth or sixth place.

After getting knocked out, I gave lots of thought to that hand and discussed it with my close friend, Tuna Lund. Our discussions changed the way that I will play this hand in similar situations. Now in this same situation, I will just smooth call the all-in bet to invite the A-K into the pot. I would like to thank my good friends Tuna Lund, Jack Fox, Vince Burgio, Eric Holum and Tom McEvoy, my writing partner, for always being available for discussions of our favorite game.

You can ask Tom and I your poker questions by registering at *www.pokerbooks.com.* Or you can e-mail us at *brad@pokerbooks.com* or *tom@pokerbooks.com.*

OPPORTUNITY #8:

Deal 100 Hands at Home

Have you ever wondered which hand is the favorite in certain situations? Suppose you want to know how one hand will stack up against another hand at the river. Is there an easy way to see which one will win after the flop?

For example, let's say that you want to know how it comes out when one player flops a set, and his opponent flops an open-end straight flush draw with neither of them getting any help on the turn card. How often will the set win on the river? How often will the flush draw win on the river? Here's how you go about it with just a deck of cards.

First, deal out the two hands that you are curious about. For starters, deal the K♠ Q♠ to Player A and deal the J♣ J♦ to Player B.

Now deal three cards in the middle of the table—the flop—plus the turn card, to make a board of four cards.

Player A   Player B

Now deal four board cards that will give Player A the flush draw and Player B the top set.

You can find out who is the favorite by simply dealing through the rest of the deck and turning up one card at a time in the middle, as though it were the river card. Every time the K♠ Q♠ wins on the river, put the river card face down in a stack in front of that hand. Every time the J♣ J♦ wins a hand, put the river card face down in a stack in front of that hand.

At the end of this simulation, you will find that the winning pile for the set of jacks will have thirty-two cards in it, and the winning pile for the K-Q will have thirteen cards. This is a good way to practice reading hands with just a deck of cards. If you prefer a faster way, computer software programs are available that can run simulations very quickly to see which hand is the favorite. For free use of one of the simulation programs, visit *www.cardplayer.com*. We thank Steve Brecher, a software developer and poker player from Reno, for offering our readers his freeware program. You can access this easy-to-use Dos software at *www.brecware.com/software/software.html*.

After the turn, how many "outs" does the K♠ Q♠ have? An out is a card that will make your hand. The K-Q has seven flush cards, two of which will give him a straight flush, three aces (in addition to the A♠) and three nines (in addition to the 9♠) will give him a straight.

Therefore, Player A has thirteen outs going into the river. How many outs does Player B have? He already has the nuts unless Player A hits one of his outs—in this sense, an out" actually is a card that will turn a losing hand into a winning hand.

Another way you can have fun and learn at the same time is to deal out nine hold'em hands. Then turn up three cards in the middle of the table. Starting with the player under the gun (the first player to the left of the big blind), decide whether he will bet or fold on the flop. Then make playing decisions for each player around the table. You might also decide which hand you would prefer holding on the flop. Then act for all of your "opponents" and deal the hand through the river.

OPPORTUNITY #9:

Keep a Poker Diary

Think of playing poker as a pleasurable business venture. Just like any other business, keeping a log with records of your daily activities and results is important. Looking at your results in cold black-and-white, you will be better able to determine what weaknesses you have and need to work on. You also can see the areas in which you are strong so that you can capitalize on your strengths. Most players find that records don't lie.

You might ask, "What do I need to record?" Keep track of the date you played, where you played, the size of the game, and notes about players in the game. Then record your win or loss for that session or tournament. At online casinos you can keep notes on players in the program's software, making it much easier to keep track of your opponents' playing styles.

OPPORTUNITY #10:

Other Ways to Improve Your Game

Naturally, we believe that reading instructional poker books is a fine way to improve your game. If tournaments are your main interest, start with *Poker Tournament Tips from the Pros* (by Shane Smith), followed by *Championship Tournament Poker* (by Tom McEvoy). Of course, we think that you also should read *Championship Satellite Strategy*, which shows you how to win cheap seats in tournaments. We also heartily recommend Bob Ciaffone's *Improve Your Poker* if you are an experienced player. If you play most of your poker online, try the online poker books by John Vorhaus and Lou Krieger.

Another way you can improve your game is by "sitting behind" a professional player in a cash game, or "sweating" a pro in a tournament. With the pro's permission, you can pull up a chair behind him during a session and observe how he plays the game, asking questions away from the table. Sweating a player in a tournament means that you observe him (and root for him, of course) throughout the course of a tournament. Take a few notes on plays that you want to ask him about later.

You also can take a tip from people in the business world who have those "power lunches." Take a professional player to lunch to discuss your poker questions in a relaxed atmosphere. He may ask for a fee in addition to your picking up the tab, but his advice usually will be well worth it.

Some professional players also accept students. Taking lessons from someone who is a winner and an acknowledged expert on poker can put you on the fast track to joining him in the winners' circle. Cardsmith Publishing authors who give poker lessons include Tom McEvoy, Brad Daugherty, T.J. Cloutier, and Roy West.

Glossary of Poker Terms

Compiled and written by Dana Smith
with Tom McEvoy & Brad Daugherty

One of the distinguishing characteristics of any profession is its language, the unique set of words that its practitioners use in describing the functions they perform. Poker professionals have a distinct language that they use to communicate with each other. Poker players don't say, "I made three cards of the same rank when the dealer spread the first three community cards." They say, "I flopped trips." Nor do they complain about "having my four aces topped by a straight flush on the last card." To them, it is "suffering a bad beat on the river."

The following glossary is a universal list of expressions that you will hear in cardrooms around the world.

All in. Betting all the chips or cash you have left in your stack. "When T.J. raised, I went *all in* with pocket kings. Unfortunately, he called my *all-in* bet with pocket aces and sent me to the rail."

Add on. The final rebuy that you can make at the end of the rebuy period in rebuy tournaments. "I only *add on* when I think that it will make my stack more competitive."

Behind you (sitting). Any player who can act after you do. "Sometimes, before you make a move to try to steal the pot, look to see who is *sitting behind you.*"

Bluff. Betting with an inferior hand in the hope of stealing the pot. "The cowboy's *bluff* with nothing-cards drove Alto out of the pot at the championship table in 1984."

Bully. A player who raises a lot of pots in an effort to make other players fold their hands. "My opponents weren't going to be easily *bullied,* so I didn't want to do a lot of aggressive raising."

Buy-in. The amount of money it costs you to enter a tournament. Usually, the larger the buy-in, the tougher the competition. "I wanted to *buy into* the championship event, but the *buy-in* was about $9,000 more than I could afford."

Case chips. Your last chips. "It took my *case chips* to call Sexton's raise on the river."

Case (ace). The last card of that rank in the deck. "When the *case ace* came on the river, Dana made a full house to beat Tom's nut flush."

Change gears. Shifting your level of aggressiveness from low gear all the way up to high gear, as though you were changing gears while driving a car. "I had to slow down and *change gears* in order to survive the late stage of the Four Queens Classic championship event."

Check. You choose not to bet. If someone sitting behind you bets, you must either call the bet, raise, or fold your cards. "When everybody *checked* the flop to Amir, he raised with a 7-6 offsuit. They all folded, and he scooped in the pot."

Check-raise. You check with a good hand in the hope of raising if someone bets. "After the flop, Daniel checked to Jeff, who made a modest bet. Daniel then *check-raised* him with pocket aces."

Chip status. A comparison of the amount of chips you have in relation to how many chips your opponents have. "At the start of the 2000 World Series of Poker championship table, T.J. was dead last in *chip status*. He moved up four spot to finish second to Chris Ferguson."

Cold call. Call a raise without having already put the initial bet into the pot. "When Jack *cold called* after Tuna reraised, Brad knew he was in trouble."

Come over the top. Raise or reraise an opponent's bet. "Some players like to *come over the top* to try to steal the pot."

Commit. Put in so many chips that you cannot turn back. You're going to play your hand to the river. "If I think the odds are in my favor, I will *fully commit*."

Counterfeit. The board pairs your key low card in Omaha high-low, demoting the value of your hand. "My A-2-6-Q got *counterfeited* when the board came 2-4-J."

Dog. Poker slang meaning that your hand is the underdog. "When I looked at Catherine's two kings at the showdown, I knew that my 10-9 offsuit was a big *dog*."

Double through. Going all-in against an opponent in order to double your stack if you win the hand. "I was so low on chips, I knew I had to *double through* somebody to build up my stack."

Flat call. Call an opponent's bet rather than raising. "Trying to trap Don, I just *flat called* the raise with my trip nines."

Get away from your hand. To decide it isn't worth it to play a hand and fold. "After Tight Ted reraised, I decided *to get away from* my hand."

Get the right price. The odds are mathematically favorable for calling. "After six players limped into the pot, Tom was *getting the right price* to call the extra $25 from the small blind."

Get full value. Betting, raising and reraising in order to manipulate the size of the pot so that you'll be getting maximum pot odds if you win the hand. "After raising on every round, I was able to *get full value* when my hand held up on the river."

Get there. Make your hand. "What happens when you don't *get there*, when you miss your hand? You cry a little."

Give action. Betting, calling, raising or reraising. Also, giving someone a gamble. "Be cautious about *giving too much action* if your kicker is weak."

Give up your hand. Fold. "I *gave up my hand* when he raised."

Gutshot. The card that completes an inside-straight draw. If you hold a 9-8 and the board is showing 10-6-2, you need a 7 to complete the straight. "In the small blind, I was all in with a 9-8. On the 10-6-2 flop, I had a *gutshot* draw at a straight. The 7 on the river made my day!"

In the dark. You don't look at your hole cards. "Tuna was so low on chips when he bet, Jack called him *in the dark*."

Ignorant end. The low end of a straight. If you have a 6-5 in your hand and the board cards are showing 9-8-7, you have the lower of two possible straights. The common axiom in poker is to avoid drawing to a lower straight when a higher one also is possible. "I got punished by a higher straight when I drew to the *ignorant end* of it. Then I kicked myself for making such an elementary blunder."

Kamikaze. A very aggressive player. Someone who seems to just close his eyes and shove his chips into the pot. "When the *kamikaze* in seat four capped the pot, my cards flew into the muck."

Key Card. The one card that will make your hand. "I knew I needed to catch a deuce, the *key card* I needed to win."

Key Hand. The hand in a tournament that proves to be a turning point, for better or worse. "There is usually one *key hand* which, if you make it, will win the tournament for you. Unfortunately, it also goes the other way."

Kicker. The sidecard you hold in hold'em, the strength of which often determines who wins in a showdown. "I had a gorgeous hand, an A-Q with an ace showing on the board. But my beauty turned into a beast when Dana showed her A-K at the river to beat me with a better *kicker*."

Lay down your hand. Fold. "Sometimes you have to *lay down your hand* because it gets too expensive to play it."

Lead. You are the first one to enter the pot. "Jack loves to *lead* into the raiser from the blind."

Level. In tournaments, the round that you are playing. A tournament level is defined by the size of the blinds. "At the $50-$100 *level*, I had only $800 in chips."

Limp (in). Enter the pot for the minimum bet (the size of the big blind). "You might decide to just *limp in* with a pair of jacks and see the flop cheaply."

Limper. A player who enters a pot for the minimum bet. "With two *limpers* in the pot, a pair of jacks should be your minimum raising hand."

Make a move. Try to bluff. "When Phil *made a move* at the pot, Huck called him down."

Maniac. A very aggressive player who sometimes plays hands his more sensible or conservative opponents would not consider. "*Maniacs* sometimes crash and burn earlier than they should in tournament play."

Mini-raise. In no-limit hold'em, you raise the minimum amount allowed, which is double the size of the big blind. "When Nguyen made a *mini-raise* from up front, I wondered whether he was trying to disguise a big hand, or just wanted to get into the pot cheaply."

Nuts. The best possible hand. "Nani won the pot when the A♣ fell on the river, giving her the *nut* flush."

On-Land Tournament. A tournament that is played in a traditional land-based casino such as Foxwoods in Connecticut. "When online poker whiz Chris Moneymaker won the World Championship of Poker in 2003, it was the first time he had ever played in an *on-land tournament.*"

Online Tournament. A tournament that is hosted by an Internet cardroom such as UltimateBet.com. "Yesterday I played a PartyPoker.com *online tournament* on my laptop while I was lounging poolside at the Golden Nugget."

Out(s). Cards that will improve your hand. "When they turned their cards face up on the turn, Duane showed three kings and Peggy showed trip aces. 'I only have one *out* to win,' Duane lamented."

Overbet. You make a raise in no-limit hold'em that is larger than normal. "Some new players who don't understand how much to bet in no-limit hold'em often *overbet* the pot."

Payout. The prize distribution in a tournament. "The *payout* for first place was 38 percent of the prize pool."

Play back. Responding to an opponent's bet by either raising or reraising. "If a tight opponent *plays back* at you, you know he probably holds the nuts."

Play fast. Always betting or raising. "Many players *play fast* in the early rounds of rebuy tournaments to try to build their stacks."

Play with. Staying in the hand by betting, calling, raising, or reraising. "I wasn't sure exactly where he was at, so I decided to *play with* him on the turn."

Position (chip position). How your chip stack compares to the stacks of your opponents. "Going into the final two tables, Brad was in tenth *chip position.* Then he went on a rush and wound up winning the whole enchilada."

Position (table position). Where you are sitting in relation to the big blind. For example, if you are sitting one seat to the left of the big blind, you are in first position. "Eric was sitting in *middle position* with a K-J offsuit when Phil raised from a *front position.* Figuring Phil for a stronger hand than K-J, Eric wisely folded."

Position (have position on). You can act after someone else acts. For example, if you are sitting on the button in a hold'em game, you have position on your opponents. "I limped into the pot because Mad Max had *position on* me and I didn't want to get into too much trouble in case he decided to raise."

Positional raise. A raise that is based more on a player's table position than on the value of his cards. "Sure, I admit that it was just a *positional raise*, but it seemed right at the time."

Pot-logged. You have so many of your chips already invested in the pot that you are committed to going to the river with your hand. "When I called Dewey's reraise, I knew I'd be going all the way with my hand. What else could I do? By then, I was *pot-logged.*"

Rag (or blank). A card that doesn't help you. "The next card was a 4♠, a total *blank.*"

Ragged(y) flop. The cards in the flop are ones that do not appear to be able to help anyone's hand; i.e., there are no straight, flush, face cards, or pairs on board. "When the flop came *raggedy* with a 7-4-2, I knew Tight Ted didn't have any part of it."

Rail. The place from which spectators and losers watch the action. "When Brad made his flush at the river to beat my set of aces, I was forced to join the other losers on the *rail*."

Raise. Increase the bet. In limit hold'em, the amount that you can raise is prescribed, but in no-limit hold'em, you can raise any amount you want so long as you raise at least twice the size of the big blind. "When you get to the final table, you seldom just call. It's either *raise* or fold."

Read (your opponents). You can determine what your opponent is holding, or the significance of his betting strategy. "His play was so erratic, it was hard to *get a read* on him."

Read (the board). You understand how the board cards in hold'em relate to your hole cards. "You must be able to *read the board* well enough to tell whether you have the nuts or nothing at all, whether you have 16 outs or no outs."

Rebuy. In rebuy tournaments, you can add chips to your stack by rebuying during a specified time period. "Before the end of the *rebuy* period, I had made three *rebuys*."

Reraise. Raise the player who raised you. Sometimes there is more than one reraise during a hand. When the maximum number of reraises have been made, the pot has been capped. "Tom knew that Brad was trying to steal his blind by raising from the button, so he *reraised* him in defense."

Ring game. A cash game, not a tournament. "The side action *ring games* during tournaments can be lucrative."

Rise. A term that refers to the increase of the blinds at the start of a new round or level of a tournament. "I knew the blinds would *rise* in three minutes, so I played a marginal hand while they were still at the lower amounts."

Rock. A very conservative player who always waits for premium cards before he plays a hand. "Smith was playing like a *rock*, so when she bet into me, I knew she had me beat."

Round. Every time the button goes completely around the table. "I just sat through three dry *rounds* where I had to fold every hand."

Run over. Playing aggressively in an attempt to control the other players. "Everyone was playing scared trying to make the money, so it was easy for Daniel to *run over* them."

Rush. A winning streak during which you might win four out of six hands, for example. "Robert is one lucky so-and-so. If he hadn't gone on that *rush* at the final table, I would've busted him in eight place."

Satellite. A preliminary tournament in which you can win a seat for a more expensive tournament. "Brad won an $80 buy-in *satellite* online at PokerStars.com that awarded an entry into a $650 buy-in super satellite." To be continued: see "super satellite."

Semi-bluff. You bet with a hand that probably isn't the best one at the moment, but which has a chance of improving. If everyone folds, your semi-bluff wins the pot for you; if someone calls, you still have a decent chance of winning. "Don's *semi-bluff* bet with only two overcards to the flop paid off when he caught an ace on the turn."

Slow down. Discontinue playing aggressively. "If Maniac Mike doesn't *slow down* in the late stage and start playing more conservatively, he's probably going to lose all those tournament chips he won with his early, aggressive play."

Smooth-call. You call rather than raise an opponent's bet. "Herb *smooth-called* me on the flop, but raised on the turn with his trip jacks."

Solid (player). A well-grounded player who thoroughly understands the game and plays it at a superior level. "You can depend on Knox to never get out of line. He's a *solid* player who always knows where he's at in a hand."

Splash around. Playing a lot of pots. "Loose Louie *splashed around* too much with a big chip lead and went broke."

Stack. All of your chips. "I just don't have the temperament to play no-limit hold'em," Timid Tony said. "I can't bear the thought of possibly losing my whole *stack* at one time."

Stage. A tournament term that refers to a particular period during a tournament. Players usually think of a tournament as having an early stage (the first three rounds), a middle stage (when about half the field has been eliminated), and a late stage, when only about three or four tables are left in action (out of a starting field of 40 tables, for example). "I caught three premium hands in the *middle stage* of the tournament, but I just couldn't hang onto them and bombed out in the *late stage* about three places out of the money."

Super Satellite. A preliminary tournament in which you can win a seat for a major tournament. Super satellites usually have 10 or more tables of players, and award as many seats into the main event as the satellite prize pool will cover. "After winning a smaller satellite, Brad won the big *super satellite* and was awarded a Caribbean cruise plus entry into the $8,000 main tournament on board ship. What a life!"

Survival (mode). Fighting to say alive in a tournament when you are very shortstacked. "It was against my basic nature to shift into *survival mode*," Action Al said, "but I wanted to hang on long enough to give myself a chance to get lucky, as Tom McEvoy advised in his book, *Championship Tournament Poker.*"

Take off a card. Calling a single bet in order to see one more card. "Tuna decided to *take off a card* to see if he could hit his inside-straight draw."

Tell. A playing habit or personal mannerism that a player consistently displays that enables his opponents to tell what he is holding or what he is likely to do during the play of a hand. "I noticed that every time Jake the Snake raised from early position with a weak hand, he sort of wobbled his chips into the pot, so I used his *tell* against him and reraised."

Throw away (a hand). Fold. "If Action Al raises from middle position, you might call with a K-Q, but if Solid Sam raises, you're probably better off to *throw your hand away.*"

Throwing a party. Several loose or amateur players are making significant monetary contributions to the game. "You have to stay in the game when they're *throwing a party.*"

Trap. You play deceptively in order to induce an unwise response from your opponent(s). "When Devious David limped into the pot from first position, I could small a *trap.* Turns out I was right: Loose Louie raised and David come over the top for all his chips."

Wake up with a hand. You are dealt a hand with winning potential. "It looked to me like Daugherty *woke up with a hand* in the small blind."

Where you're at. You know the value of your hand compared to your opponent's hand. "Hamid may have raised just to find out *where he was at.*"

World's fair. A very big hand. "Suppose the flop comes with 8-8-4 in different suits. You know you're either up against nothing or *the world's fair*."

GREAT CARDOZA POKER BOOKS
ADD THESE TO YOUR LIBRARY - ORDER NOW!

WINNER'S GUIDE TO TEXAS HOLD' EM POKER *by Ken Warren* - The most comprehensive book on beating hold 'em shows serious players how to play every hand from every position with every type of flop. Learn the 14 categories of starting hands, the 10 most common Hold'em tells, how to evaluate a game for profit, value of deception, art of bluffing, 8 secrets to winning, starting hand categories, position, more! Bonus: Includes detailed analysis of the top 40 hands and the most complete chapter on hold'em odds in print. Over 50,000 copies in print. 224 pages, 5 1/2 x 8 1/2, paperback, $14.95.

KEN WARREN TEACHES TEXAS HOLD 'EM *by Ken Warren* - This is a step-by-step comprehensive manual for making money at hold 'em poker. 42 powerful chapters teach you one lesson at a time. Great practical advice and concepts with examples from actual games and how to apply them to your own play. Lessons include: Starting Cards, Playing Position, Raising, Check-raising, Tells, Game/Seat Selection, Dominated Hands, Odds, much more. This book is already a huge fan favorite and best-seller! 416 pgs. $26.95

WINNER'S GUIDE TO OMAHA POKER *by Ken Warren* - In a concise and easy-to-understand style, Warren shows beginning and intermediate Omaha players how to win from the first time they play. You'll learn the rules, betting and blind structure, why to play Omaha, the advantages of Omaha over Texas Hold'em, glossary, reading the board, basic strategies, Omaha high, Omaha hi-low split 8/better, how to play draws and made hands, evaluation of starting hands, counting outs, computing pot odds, the unique characteristics of split-pot games, the best and worst Omaha hands, how to play before the flop, how to play on the flop, how to play on the turn and river and much more. 224 pgs. $19.95

POKER WISDOM OF A CHAMPION *by Doyle Brunson* - Learn what it takes to be a great poker player by climbing inside the mind of poker's most famous champion. Fascinating anecdotes and adventures from Doyle's early career playing poker in roadhouses and with other great champions are interspersed with lessons one can learn from the champion who has made more money at poker than anyone else in the history of the game. Readers learn what makes a great player tick, how he approaches the game, and receive candid, powerful advice from the legend himself. The Mad Genius of poker, Mike Caro, says, "Brunson is the greatest poker player who ever lived . This book shows why." 192 pgs. $14.95.

BOBBY BALDWIN'S WINNING POKER SECRETS *by Mike Caro with Bobby Baldwin*. New edition—now back in print! This is the fascinating account of 1978 World Champion Bobby Baldwin's early career playing poker in roadhouses and against other poker legends and his meteoric rise to the championship. It is interspersed with important lessons on what makes a great player tick and how he approaches the game. Baldwin and Mike Caro, both of whom are co-authors of the classic Doyle Brunson's Super System, cover the common mistakes average players make at seven poker variations and the dynamic winning concepts they must employ to win. Endorsed by poker legends and superstars Doyle Brunson and Amarillo Slim. 208 pages, 5 1/2 x 8 1/2, paperback, $14.95.

POKER TOURNAMENT TIPS FROM THE PROS *by Shane Smith* - Essential advice from poker theorists, authors, and tournament winners on the best strategies for winning the big prizes at low-limit re-buy tournaments. Learn the best strategies for each of the four stages of play–opening, middle, late and final–how to avoid 26 potential traps, advice on re-buys, aggressive play, clock-watching, inside moves, top 20 tips for winning tournaments, more. Advice from McEvoy, Caro, Malmuth, Ciaffone, others. 160 pages, 5 1/2 x 8 1/2, $19.95.

HOW TO WIN AT OMAHA HIGH-LOW POKER *by Mike Cappelletti* - Clearly written strategies and powerful advice shows the essential winning strategies for beating the hottest new casino poker game—Omaha high-low poker! This money-making guide includes more than sixty hard-hitting sections on Omaha. Players learn the rules of play, best starting hands, strategies for the flop, turn, and river, how to read the board for both high and low, dangerous draws, and how to beat low-limit tournaments. Includes odds charts, glossary, low-limit tips, strategic ideas. 304 pgs, $19.95.

GREAT CARDOZA POKER BOOKS
ADD THESE TO YOUR LIBRARY - ORDER NOW!

HOW TO BEAT LOW-LIMIT 7 CARD STUD POKER *by Paul Kammen* - Written for low-limit and first time players, you'll learn the different hands that can be played, the correct bets to make, and how to tailor strategies for maximum profits. Tons of information includes spread-limit and fixed-limit game, starting hands, 3rd-7th street strategy, overcards, psychology and much more. 192 pgs. $14.95.

OMAHA HI-LO POKER *by Shane Smith* - Learn essential winning strategies for beating Omaha high-low; the best starting hands, how to play the flop, turn, and river, how to read the board for both high and low, dangerous draws, and how to win low-limit tournaments. Smith shows the differences between Omaha high-low and hold'em strategies. Includes odds charts, glossary, low-limit tips, strategic ideas. 84 pages, 8 x 11, spiral bound, $17.95.

7-CARD STUD (THE COMPLETE COURSE IN WINNING AT MEDIUM & LOWER LIMITS) *by Roy West* - Learn the latest strategies for winning at $1-$4 spread-limit up to $10-$20 fixed-limit games. Covers starting hands, 3rd-7th street strategy for playing most hands, overcards, selective aggressiveness, reading hands, secrets of the pros, psychology, more in a 42 lesson informal format. Includes bonus chapter on 7-stud tournament strategy by World Champion Tom McEvoy. 160 pages, paperback, $24.95.

WINNING LOW LIMIT HOLD'EM *by Lee Jones* - This essential book on playing 1-4, 3-6, and 1-4-8-8 low limit hold'em is packed with insights on winning: pre-flop positional play; playing the flop in all positions with a pair, two pair, trips, overcards, draws, made and nothing hands; turn and river play; how to read the board; avoiding trash hands; using the check-raise; bluffing, stereotypes, much more. Includes quizzes with answers. Terrific book. 176 pages, 5 1/2 x 8 1/2, paperback, $19.95.

BIG BOOK OF POKER *by Ken Warren* - This easy-to-read and oversized guide teaches you everything you need to know to win money at home poker, and in cardrooms, casinos and on the tournament circuit. Readers will learn how to bet, raise, and checkraise, bluff, semi-bluff, and how to take advantage of position and pot odds. Great sections on hold'em (plus, stud games, Omaha, draw games, and many more) and playing and winning poker on the internet. Packed with charts, diagrams, sidebars, and detailed, easy-to-read examples by best-selling poker expert Ken Warren, this wonderfully formatted book is one stop shopping for players ready to take on any form of poker for real money. Want to be a big player? Buy the Big Book of Poker! 320 oversized pgs, $19.95.

WINNING POKER FOR THE SERIOUS PLAYER *by Edwin Silberstang* - More than 100 actual examples and tons of advice on beating 7 Card Stud, Texas Hold 'Em, Draw Poker, Loball, High-Low and 10 other variations. Silberstang analyzes the essentials of being a great player; reading tells, analyzing tables, playing position, mastering the art of deception, creating fear at the table. Also, psychological tactics, when to play aggressive or slow play, or fold, expert plays, more. Colorful glossary included. 304 pages, 6 x 9, $16.95.

HOW TO PLAY WINNING POKER *by Avery Cardoza* - New and expanded edition shows playing and winning strategies for all major games: five & seven stud games, Omaha, draw poker, hold'em, and high-low, both for home and casino play. You'll learn 15 winning poker concepts, how to minimize losses and maximize profits, how to read opponents and gain the edge against their style, how to use use pot odds, tells, position, more. 160 pgs. $12.95

We have new poker books coming out all the time.
To see our full range of poker titles, visit our web site:

cardozapub.com

FROM CARDSMITH'S EXCITING LIBRARY
ADD THESE TO YOUR COLLECTION - ORDER NOW!

NO-LIMIT TEXAS HOLD 'EM: The New Player's Guide to Winning Poker's Biggest Game *by Brad Daugherty & Tom McEvoy.* For experienced limit players who want to play no-limit or rookies who has never played before, two world champions give readers a crash course in how to join the elite ranks of million-dollar, no-limit hold'em tournament winners and cash game players. Readers learn the winning principles and four major skills: how to evaluate the strength of a hand, determine how much to bet, how to understand opponents' play, and how to bluff and when to do it. 74 game scenarios, two unique betting charts for tournament play and sections on essential principles and strategies, show you how to get to the winners' circle. Special section on beating online tournaments. 288 pages, $24.95.

COWBOYS, GAMBLERS & HUSTLERS: The True Adventures of a Rodeo Champion & Poker Legend by *Byron "Cowboy" Wolford.* Ride along with the road gamblers as they fade the white line from Dallas to Shreveport to Houston in the 1960s in search of a score. Feel the fear and frustration of being hijacked, getting arrested for playing poker, and having to outwit card sharps and scam artists. Wolford survived it all to win a WSOP gold bracelet playing with poker greats Amarillo Slim Preston, Johnny Moss and Bobby Baldwin (and 30 rodeo belt buckles). Read fascinating yarns about life on the rough and tumble, and colorful adventures as a road gambler and hustler gambling in smoky backrooms with legends Titanic Thompson, Jack Straus, Doyle Brunson and get a look at vintage Las Vegas when Cowboy's friend, Benny Binion ruled Glitter Gulch. Read about the most famous bluff in WSOP history. Endorsed by Jack Binion, Doyle Brunson & Bobby Baldwin, who says, *Cowboy is probably the best gambling story teller in the world.* 304 pages, $19.95.

SECRETS OF WINNING POKER by *Tex Sheahan.* This is a compilation of Sheahan's best articles from 15 years of writing for the major gaming magazines as his legacy to poker players. Sheahan gives you sound advice on winning poker strategies for hold'em and 7-card stud. Chapters on tournament play, psychology, personality profiles and some very funny stories from the greenfelt jungle. "Some of the best advice you'll ever read on how to win at poker" -- Doyle Brunson. 200 pages, paperback. Originally $19.95, now only $14.95.

OMAHA HI-LO: Play to Win with the Odds by *Bill Boston.* Selecting the right hands to play is the most important decision you'll make in Omaha high-low poker. In this book you'll find the odds for every hand dealt in Omaha high-low—the chances that the hand has of winning the high end of the pot, the low end of it, and how often it is expected to scoop the whole pot. The results are based on 10,000 simulations for each one of the possible 5,211 Omaha high-low hands. Boston has organized the data into an easy-to-use format and added insights learned from years of experience. Learn the 5,211 Omaha high-low hands, the 49 best hands and their odds, the 49 worst hands, trap hands to avoid, and 30 Ace-less hands you can play for profit. A great tool for Omaha players! 156 pages, $19.95.

OMAHA HI-LO POKER (8 OR BETTER): How to win at the lower limits *by Shane Smith.* Since its first printing in 1991, this has become the classic in the field for low-limit players. Readers have lauded the author's clear and concise writing style. Smith shows you how to put players on hands, read the board for high and low, avoid dangerous draws, and use winning betting strategies. Chapters include starting hands, the flop, the turn, the river, and tournament strategy. Illustrated with pictorials of sample hands, an odds chart, and a starting hands chart. Lou Krieger, author of *Poker for Dummies,* says, *Shane Smith's book is terrific! If you're new to Omaha high-low split or if you're a low-limit player who wants to improve your game, you ought to have this book in your poker library. Complex concepts are presented in an easy-to-understand format. It's a gem!* 82 pages, spiralbound. $17.95.

THE WACKY SIDE OF POKER *by Ralph E. Wheeler.* Take a walk on the wacky side with 88 humorous poker cartoons! Also includes 220 wise and witty poker quotes. Lighten up from all the heavy reading and preparation of the games wit a quick walk through this fun book. Perfect for holiday gifting. 176 pages filled with wit and wisdom will bring a smile to your face. At less than a ten-spot, you can't go wrong! 176 pages, $9.95.

Order Toll-Free 1-800-577-WINS or use order form on page 286

THE CHAMPIONSHIP SERIES
POWERFUL BOOKS YOU **MUST** HAVE

CHAMPIONSHIP TOURNAMENT POKER *by Tom McEvoy*. New Cardoza Edition! Rated by pros as best book on tournaments ever written and enthusiastically endorsed by more than 5 world champions, this is the definitive guide to winning tournaments and a *must* for every player's library. McEvoy lets you in on the secrets he has used to win millions of dollars in tournaments and the insights he has learned competing against the best players in the world. Packed solid with winning strategies for all 11 games in the *World Series of Poker*, with extensive discussions of 7-card stud, limit hold'em, pot and no-limit hold'em, Omaha high-low, re-buy, half-half tournaments, satellites, strategies for each stage of tournaments. Tons of essential concepts and specific strategies jam-pack the book. Phil Hellmuth, 1989 WSOP champion says, *[this] is the world's most definitive guide to winning poker tournaments.* 416 pages, paperback, $29.95.

CHAMPIONSHIP TABLE (at the World Series of Poker) *by Dana Smith, Ralph Wheeler, and Tom McEvoy.* New Cardoza Edition! From 1970 when the champion was presented a silver cup, to the present when the champion was awarded more than $2 million, Championship Table celebrates three decades of poker greats who have competed to win poker's most coveted title. This book gives you the names and photographs of all the players who made the final table, pictures the last hand the champion played against the runner-up, how they played their cards, and how much they won. There is also features fascinating interviews and conversations with the champions and runners-up and interesting highlights from each Series. This is a fascinating and invaluable resource book for WSOP and gaming buffs. In some cases the champion himself wrote "how it happened," as did two-time champion Doyle Brunson when Stu Ungar caught a wheel in 1980 on the turn to deprive "Texas Dolly" of his third title. Includes tons of vintage photographs. 208 pages, paperback, $19.95.

CHAMPIONSHIP SATELLITE STRATEGY *by Brad Dougherty & Tom McEvoy.* In 2002 and 2003 satellite players won their way into the $10,000 WSOP buy-in and emerged as champions, winning more than $2 million each. You can too! You'll learn specific, proven strategies for winning almost any satellite. Learn the 10 ways to win a seat at the WSOP and other big tournaments, how to win limit hold'em and no-limit hold'em satellites, one-table satellites for big tournaments, and online satellites, plus how to play the final table of super satellites. McEvoy and Daugherty sincerely believe that if you practice these strategies, you can win your way into any tournament for a fraction of the buy-in. You'll learn how much to bet, how hard to pressure opponents, how to tell when an opponent is bluffing, how to play deceptively, and how to use your chips as weapons of destruction. Includes a special chapter on no-limit hold'em satellites! 256 pages. illustrated hands, photos, glossary. $24.95.

CHAMPIONSHIP PRACTICE HANDS *by T. J. Cloutier & Tom McEvoy.* Two tournament legends show you how to become a winning tournament player. Get inside their heads as they think they way through the correct strategy at 57 limit and no-limit practice hands. Cloutier & McEvoy show you how to use your skill and intuition to play strategic hands for maximum profit in real tournament scenarios and how 45 key hands were played by champions in turnaround situations at the WSOP. By sharing their analysis on how the winners and losers played key hands, you'll gain tremendous insights into how tournament poker is played at the highest levels. Learn how champions think and how they play major hands in strategic tournament situations, Cloutier and McEvoy believe that you will be able to win your share of the profits in today's tournaments -- and join them at the championship table far sooner than you ever imagined. 288 pages, illustrated with card pictures, $29.95

THE CHAMPIONSHIP SERIES
POWERFUL BOOKS YOU __MUST__ HAVE

CHAMPIONSHIP HOLD'EM *by T. J. Cloutier & Tom McEvoy.* Hard-hitting hold'em the way it's played *today* in both limit cash games and tournaments. Get killer advice on how to win more money in rammin'-jammin' games, kill-pot, jackpot, shorthanded, and other types of cash games. You'll learn the thinking process before the flop, on the flop, on the turn, and at the river with specific suggestions for what to do when good or bad things happen plus 20 illustrated hands with play-by-play analyses. Specific advice for rocks in tight games, weaklings in loose games, experts in solid games, how hand values change in jackpot games, when you should fold, check, raise, reraise, check-raise, slowplay, bluff, and tournament strategies for small buy-in, big buy-in, rebuy, incremental add-on, satellite and big-field major tournaments. Wow! Easy-to-read and conversational, if you want to become a lifelong winner at limit hold'em, you need this book! 320 Pages, Illustrated, Photos. $39.95

CHAMPIONSHIP NO-LIMIT & POT-LIMIT HOLD'EM *by T. J. Cloutier & Tom McEvoy*
New Cardoza edition! This is the bible of winning pot-limit and no-limit hold'em tournaments, the definitive guide to winning at two of the world's most exciting poker games! Written by eight-time World Champion players T.J. Cloutier (1998 *and* 2002 Player of the Year) and Tom McEvoy (the foremost author on tournament strategy) who have won millions of dollars each playing no-limit and pot-limit hold'em in cash games and major tournaments around the world. You'll get all the answers here —no holds barred—to your most important questions: How do you get inside your opponents' heads and learn how to beat them at their own game? How can you tell how much to bet, raise, and reraise in no-limit hold'em? When can you bluff? How do you set up your opponents in pot-limit hold'em so that you can win a monster pot? What are the best strategies for winning no-limit and pot-limit tournaments, satellites, and supersatellites? Rock-solid and inspired advice from two of the most recognizable figures in poker — advice that you can bank on. If you want to become a future champion, you must have this book. 304 pages, paperback, photos. $29.95

CHAMPIONSHIP OMAHA (Omaha High-Low, Pot-limit Omaha, Limit High Omaha) *by T. J. Cloutier & Tom McEvoy.* Clearly-written strategies and powerful advice from Cloutier and McEvoy who have won four World Series of Poker titles in Omaha tournaments. Powerful advice shows you how to win at low-limit and high-stakes games, how to play against loose and tight opponents, and the differing strategies for rebuy and freezeout tournaments. Learn the best starting hands, when slowplaying a big hand is dangerous, what danglers are and why winners don't play them, why pot-limit Omaha is the only poker game where you sometimes fold the nuts on the flop and are correct in doing so and overall, how can you win a lot of money at Omaha! 230 pages, photos, illustrations, $39.95.

CHAMPIONSHIP STUD (Seven-Card Stud, Stud 8/or Better and Razz) *by Dr. Max Stern, Linda Johnson, and Tom McEvoy.* The authors, who have earned millions of dollars in major tournaments and cash games, eight World Series of Poker bracelets and hundreds of other titles in competition against the best players in the world show you the winning strategies for medium-limit side games as well as poker tournaments and a general tournament strategy that is applicable to any form of poker. Includes give-and-take conversations between the authors to give you more than one point of view on how to play poker. 200 pages, hand pictorials, photos. $29.95.

Order Toll-Free 1-800-577-WINS or use order form on page 286

POWERFUL POKER SIMULATIONS

A MUST FOR SERIOUS PLAYERS WITH A COMPUTER!
IBM compatibles CD ROM Win 95, 98, 2000, NT, ME, XP - Full Color Graphics

Play interactive poker against these **incredible** full color poker simulation programs - they're the absolute **best** method to improve game. *Computer players act like real players.* All games let you set the limits and rake, have fully programmable players, adjustable lineup, stat tracking, and Hand Analyzer for starting hands. MIke Caro, the world's foremost poker theoretician says, *"Amazing...A steal for under $500...get it, it's great."* "Includes *free telephone support.* **New Feature!** - "Smart advisor" gives expert advice for *every* play in *every* game!

1. TURBO TEXAS HOLD'EM FOR WINDOWS - $89.95 - Choose which players, how many, 2-10, you want to play, create loose/tight game, control check-raising, bluffing, position, sensitivity to pot odds, more! Also, instant replay, pop-up odds, Professional Advisor, keeps track of play statistics. Free bonus: *Hold'em Hand Analyzer* analyzes all 169 pocket hands in detail, their win rates under any conditions you set. Caro says this *"hold'em software is the most powerful ever created."* Great product!

2. TURBO SEVEN-CARD STUD FOR WINDOWS - $89.95 - *Create any conditions of play,* choose number of players (2-8), bet amounts, fixed or spread limit, bring-in method, tight/ loose conditions, position, reaction to board, number of dead cards, stack deck to create special conditions, instant replay. Terrific stat reporting includes analysis of starting cards, 3-D bar charts, graphs. Play interactively, run high speed simulation to test strategies. *Hand Analyzer* analyzes starting hands in detail. Wow!

3. TURBO OMAHA HIGH-LOW SPLIT FOR WINDOWS - $89.95 -Specify any playing conditions; betting limits, number of raises, blind structures, button position, aggressiveness/ passiveness of opponents, number of players (2-10), types of hands dealt, blinds, position, board reaction, specify flop, turn, river cards! Choose opponents, use provided point count or create your own. Statistical reporting, instant replay, pop-up odds, high speed simulation to test strategies, amazing Hand Analyzer, much more!

4. TURBO OMAHA HIGH FOR WINDOWS - $89.95 - Same features as above, but tailored for the Omaha High-only game. Caro says program is *"an electrifying research tool...it can clearly be worth thousands of dollars to any serious player.* A must for Omaha High players.

5. TURBO 7 STUD 8 OR BETTER - $89.95 - Brand new with all the features you expect from the Wilson Turbo products: the latest artificial intelligence, instant advice and exact odds, play versus 2-7 opponents, enhanced data charts that can be exported or printed, the ability to fold out of turn and immediately go to the next hand, ability to peek at opponents hand, optional warning mode that warns you if a play disagrees with the advisor, and automatic testing mode that can run up to 50 tests unattended. Challenge tough computer players who vary their styles for a truly great poker game.

---

6. TOURNAMENT TEXAS HOLD'EM - $59.95
Set-up for tournament practice and play, this realistic simulation pits you against celebrity look-alikes. Tons of options let you control tournament size with 10 to 300 entrants, select limits, ante, rake, blind structures, freezeouts, number of rebuys and competition level of opponents - average, tough, or toughest. Pop-up status report shows how you're doing vs. the competition. Save tournaments in progress to play again later. Additional feature allows you to quickly finish a folded hand and go on to the next.

VIDEOS BY MIKE CARO
THE MAD GENIUS OF POKER

CARO'S PRO POKER TELLS

The long-awaited two-video set is a powerful scientific course on how to use your opponents' gestures, words and body language to read their hands and win all their money. These carefully guarded poker secrets, filmed with 63 poker notables, will revolutionize your game. It reveals when opponents are bluffing, when they aren't, and why. Knowing what your opponent's gestures mean, and protecting them from knowing yours, gives you a huge winning edge. *An absolute must buy!* $59.95.

CARO'S MAJOR POKER SEMINAR

The legendary "Mad Genius" is at it again, giving poker advice in VHS format. This new tape is based on the inaugural class at Mike Caro University of Poker, Gaming and Life strategy. The material given on this tape is based on many fundamentals introduced in Caro's books, papers, and articles and is prepared in such a way that reinforces concepts old and new. Caro's style is easy-going but intense with key concepts stressed and repeated. This tape will improve your play. 60 Minutes. $24.95.

CARO'S POWER POKER SEMINAR

This powerful video shows you how to win big money using the little-known concepts of world champion players. This advice will be worth thousands of dollars to you every year, even more if you're a big money player! After 15 years of refusing to allow his seminars to be filmed, Caro presents entertaining but serious coverage of his long-guarded secrets. Contains the most profitable poker advice ever put on video. 62 Minutes! $39.95.

Order Toll-Free 1-800-577-WINS or use order form on page 286

CARDOZA PUBLISHING ONLINE

For the latest in poker, gambling, chess, backgammon, and games
by the world's top authorities and writers

www.cardozapub.com

To find out about our latest publications and products, to order books and software from third parties, or simply to keep aware of our latest activities in the world or poker, gambling, and other games of chance and skill:

1. Go online: www.cardozapub.com
2. Use E-Mail: cardozapub@aol.com
3. Call toll free: 800-577-WINS (800-577-9467)